AWESOME
ACTIVITY BOOK

TERRY DEARY

SCHOLASTIC

Scholastic Children's Books
Euston House
24 Eversholt Street
London
NW1 1DB

A division of Scholastic Ltd
London ~ New York ~ Toronto ~ Sydney ~ Auckland
Mexico City ~ New Delhi ~ Hong Kong

Published by Scholastic Ltd, 2007

Some of the material in this book has previously been published in
Horrible Histories: *The Awesome Egyptians*, *The Awesome Ancient Quiz Book*,
The Groovy Greeks and *The Incredible Incas*.

10 digit ISBN: 1 407 10304 0
13 digit ISBN: 978 1407 10304 4

Printed and bound by Tien Wah Press Pte. Ltd, Malaysia

2 4 6 8 10 9 7 5 3

The right of Terry Deary, Martin Brown and Philip Reeve to be identified as the
author and illustrators of the above books respectively has been asserted by them in
accordance with the Copyright, Designs and Patents Act, 1988.

Additional text by Pam Kelt, Dereen Taylor and Jenny Siklos
Additional illustrations and colour work by Stuart Martin and Mike Phillips

Activities created and produced by The Complete Works, St Mary's Road, Royal
Leamington Spa, Warwickshire CV31 1JP, UK

CONTENTS

IS THERE A CHAPTER ON FIRST AID?

WHAT IS AN AWESOME EGYPTIAN?

The awesome Egyptians weren't just fabulous pharaohs and mean mummies!
Ninety per cent of ancient Egyptians were peasants who worked very hard.
Peasants were like property – if a pharaoh gave land to a nobleman then
the peasants were thrown in as well.

There were few slaves in Egypt, but if you were a peasant you may as well have been one! Peasants were counted along with the cattle to show how rich a landowner was. Women were not counted because they were not worth as much as cattle!

Below are the peasants and cattle that work on Ali Fayed's land.
Can you find them in the picture above and work out how rich he is?

TOTAL

4   4   8   5   28

4

When the Nile was in flood, peasants were ordered to work on the pyramids. If you didn't work fast enough then you would be punished by whipping or by having bits chopped off your body – a finger or a toe, perhaps. Follow the paths to work out which peasant is going to face the chop.

A

B

C

D

Some peasants who worked hard on the pyramids suffered terrible conditions. Unscramble the words in CAPITAL LETTERS to find out what happened.

1) Workers dragged huge ~~TESON KLOCBS~~ for 60 kilometres over the GRINNUB RESTED.

Stone BLOCKS

2) They were paid with some REDAB, linen and MINTTONE.

3) At the end of the day, workers trudged back to their barracks – rough MELONSITE shelters with DUM SOFORL.

4) Rooms were ROCWDDE with no TREWA or LOITETS.

5) The barracks really KNUTS from human GASWEE and from the MANALIS that shared the space.

6) The workers wanted to go home but they knew they would die of NOTATRAVIS before they got there!

THESE CONDITIONS ARE NOT FIT FOR A PEASANT

WRITE LIKE AN EGYPTIAN

To be a top man in Egypt you had to be able to read and write. Boys (not girls) had to go to school in the temple and suffer under terrible teachers who worked them and beat them without mercy. One tough teacher said that boys needed a good beating if they were going to learn. In Egypt you had to suffer to succeed.

Egyptian writing is called hieroglyphics. Sometimes a hieroglyphic sign means a letter – the way it does in our alphabet. Sometimes it means a whole word. Hieroglyphs were deliberately complicated so that it took a long time to read and write them. It meant that those who could read and write were more important.

Here are some Egyptian hieroglyphs. Use them to write your name. The Egyptians didn't have signs for letters C, E, O, U, V and X, so you will need to add these letters with the hieroglyphs.

A. vulture

B. leg

D. hand

F. viper

G. pot or stand

CH. rope

I. reed

J. serpent

K. basket

L. lion

M. owl

N. water

P. stool

Q. hill

R. mouth

S. cloth

T. loaf

W. chick

Y. reeds

Z. bolt

FISH, HAND, SQUIGGLE SPELLS CAT

See if you can read these two messages. The sound of the letters is more important than the spelling. Anyway, who says the Egyptians had to be good at spelling? Are you?

EH?

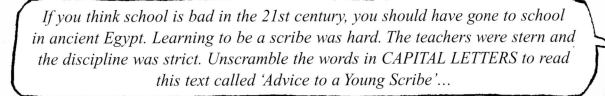

If you think school is bad in the 21st century, you should have gone to school in ancient Egypt. Learning to be a scribe was hard. The teachers were stern and the discipline was strict. Unscramble the words in CAPITAL LETTERS to read this text called 'Advice to a Young Scribe'...

O scribe do not be LIED, or you shall be CRUDES.

Do TON give your EARTH to RULES PEA or you

HALLS fail. Do not PENDS a day in SEEN LIDS or you

shall be AT BEEN. A YOB'S ear is on his DICE BASK

and he listens HEWN he is BEE TAN!

Can you find the list of these hieroglyphs hidden in the grid below? They can be found written up, down, backwards and across. Then try and work out what the hieroglyphs say. If you can, you are on the way to becoming an awesome Egyptian expert!

1)

2)

3)

4)

5)

6)

GRUESOME GODS

Egyptians wanted to reach the spirit world that the priests taught about. There was an awesome number of gods for an Egyptian to please before he or she got there. And if they annoyed one, well, it was tombs-full of trouble for them!

Egyptian gods were unbelievably old. They had lived before people existed and now treated humans as if they were a mixture of toys and servants. The gods controlled the world and everything that happened. They demanded respect. Can you match the images of the gods below to their descriptions?

A

1) Anubis – the jackal-headed god of the dead. He helped to prepare mummies.

L

2) Bes – the dwarf god of happiness, and protector of the family.

3) Hathor – the cow-horned goddess of love. She also looked after happiness, dancing and music.

4) Horus – the falcon-headed god who looked after the pharaoh.

5) Isis – wife of Osiris. She took special care of women and children.

B

6) Osiris – god of death and rebirth, the Underworld and the Earth. Long ago he had taught people to farm.

K

7) Ptah – the god who spoke the names of all the things in the world. By doing this he made them exist.

8) Re – the Sun God. Some said he had made people. The Egyptians called themselves, 'the cattle of Re'.

C

9) Seth – god of the desert and storms. The enemy of Osiris.

10) Sekhmet – the lioness goddess of war.

11) Sobek – the crocodile-headed god. He controlled water supplies.

J

12) Thoth – the ibis-headed god of wisdom who invented speaking and writing.

D

E

F

G

H

I

8

Need an awesome answer to a powerful problem? Read the Dear God… letters below and use the list of gods on page 6 to work out which god each person is praying to.

1) Oh great _Osiris_. My land is short of water and my crops are dying.
2) Mighty _Isis_. My youngest son died of fever three months ago. Since then my wife is heart-broken. Please help her to enjoy life again.
3) Oh wise _Thoth_. My son wishes to be a scribe, but he is so bad at learning his hieroglyphs that his teachers are threatening to throw him out of school. Beatings don't seem to help.
4) Please give me strength, oh vengeful _Sekhmet_. Raiders from the Red Land have attacked our village. Help us to defeat them.
5) Please, sweet _Hathor_. I am madly in love with the most beautiful girl, but she laughs at my dancing. I am terribly clumsy and fall over my own feet.

ERRR!

GO ON! DO YOU WANT TO DANCE WITH HER OR DON'T YOU!?

Most awesome Egyptian myths have various versions of the same story. Here is one version of the Isis and Osiris story. Sadly our suffering scribe has scrambled the terrible tale in places. Can you unscramble the words in CAPITAL LETTERS?

Osiris was an awesome king. He was loved by his loyal wife, Isis, and all of his people. Only Osiris's brother, Set, hated him. He was LASOUJE of his brother and planned to kill him.

Set DOINGEARS a large feast. At the height of the festivities, Set produced a casket and ACNDOENUN that it would be given to whoever it fitted. All the guests tried the casket for size, but none fitted, until finally, Osiris stepped into the casket. Set slammed the lid closed and sealed the casket shut with boiling lead. The SALDEE coffin was then thrown into the Nile.

Isis SEHCRAED for the casket all over Egypt. At last, she found it where it had come to rest in the roots of a huge tree.

Isis took the coffin back for a proper ALIRUB. For safety, she hid it in the marshes beside the Nile. Sneaky Set found the casket and was so GEDENRA he chopped the body of Osiris into pieces, and RECAEDSTT the parts throughout the land of Egypt.

Poor Isis set out again looking for the bits of her husband. At last, she found all the parts except one (his naughty bit) and reassembled Osiris and PAREDPW him in bandages. The first mummy!

Osiris was also a daddy and his son, Horus, went out to battle his savage uncle Set. After a series of battles, neither was able to win. In the end, Osiris was made king of the underworld, Horus – king of the living and Set – ruler of the deserts as the god of evil. So they all died happily ever after!

9

PHASCINATING PHARAOHS

After the Egyptians invented gods, some clever people said, 'Actually, we are those gods you pray to! So give us food, build us palaces, worship us and we'll look after you.' These clever people became known as 'pharaohs' – probably because they had a 'fair-old' life with peasants 'slaving' for them!

Pharaohs ruled for almost 3,000 years so there were bound to be a few odd ones among all that lot. If there had been newspapers in those days then imagine the headlines. But there weren't and even if there had been, they'd have been crumbly by now and key words may have fallen out. Can you add the missing words to these headlines?

Missing words, but not in the correct order:
Greek, hundred, money, goose, murder, elephants, magician, lion, woman, wrinkly.

1 SENSATION! PHARAOH HATSHEPSUT IS A _goose_

2 HORROR! IS TUTANKHAMUN A VICTIM OF _murder_?

3 SHOCK! TUT'S WIDOW, ANKHESENAMUN, MARRIES A _Greek_!

4 ASTONISHING! PEPY II HITS A _magician_!

5 WONDER! HAIR CLIP FOUND BY _woman_!

6 AMAZING! PHARAOH'S ENTERTAINER PUTS HEAD BACK ON _lion_!

7 ASTOUNDING! RAMESES II FACES ENEMY ARMY WITH JUST A _____!

8 WOW! THUTMOSE III ESCAPES BEING KILLED BY _elephant_

9 DESPICABLE! PSAMMETICHUS HOLDS OFF INVASION WITH _____!

10 EGYPTIAN SHAME! CLEOPATRA IS A _____!

I WOULDN'T LOOK UP THERE IF I WERE YOU

After ruling for 30 years, the pharaoh had to prove his fitness by running round a fixed course. This terrible trial was held at the Heb-sed festival. Can you work out which obstacle course will lead the pharaoh to the finish line?

FINISH

The carvings on all Egyptian monuments show the king as a conqueror. What if you lost? Don't worry, the scribes can still say you won! Rameses II fought the Hittites at the Battle of Qadesh in Syria. The Egyptian scribes described his victory. The Hittite scribes described the same battle – but in the Hittite story the Hittites won! Look at the two battle scenes below. Spot ten differences between the two and circle them with a pencil.

IF THIS IS WINNING, I'D HATE TO LOSE!

IF THIS IS WINNING, I'D HATE TO LOSE!

POWERFUL PYRAMIDS

Pharaohs were no different to other Egyptians. They also worried about reaching the spirit world when they died. They had huge stone tombs built. These were called pyramids. When the pharaohs died, their bodies would be safe inside a burial chamber. The pyramid contained everything the pharaoh would need in the afterlife … including a toilet.

There are some awesome things you ought to know about the pyramids. Here is a crossword with a difference – it doesn't have any clues. The words missing from the facts below make up the answers. The information in brackets tells you where they should go in the grid.

1) A pyramid was supposedly built as a huge stone _tomb_ (6 across, 4 letters) of a pharaoh.

2) The burial chamber in the centre was filled with awesome _gold_ (5 down, 6 letters) for the pharaoh to take into the afterlife.

3) The riches were a temptation to _____ (4 across, 7 letters). The pyramid builders tried to fool the thieves by making false doors, staircases and corridors.

4) The base of the Great Pyramid of Cheops is equal to the area of seven or eight _____ (3 down, 8 letters) pitches (230 metres x 230 metres).

5) The pyramids are close to the _____ (1 down, 4 letters) because some of the huge stones had to be carried from the quarries by boat.

6) The pyramids are all on the west bank of the Nile – the side on which the ___ (7 across, 3 letters) sets. This is for religious reasons.

7) The pyramids were built from enormous stone blocks. But how did the Egyptians _____ (2 across, 4 letters) them when they had no cranes?

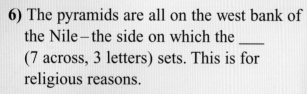

Not everyone agrees the pyramids are graves, of course. Thinking about those great lumps of dense stone, are people with great lumps of dense brains who have other ideas. But which of the following wacky ideas have some people seriously believed? Answer true or false…

Someone has said that the pyramids are…

1) Adverts. The priests wanted to leave something to show the world how great they were.

2) Simple landmarks. All maps would be drawn with the pyramids at the centre and distances worked out from there.

3) Chambers of horrors. Dead kings were stuck inside, then the Egyptian people were charged two onions an hour to walk around and view their kingly corpses.

4) Sundials. The shadow from the Great Pyramid would be used to work out the time.

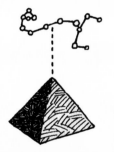

5) Mathematical horoscopes. They've been used to predict the birth of Christ, the date of World War 1 and the end of the world – AD 2979 if you're worried.

6) Star calculators. They help to measure the speed of light, the distance from the earth to the sun and to keep a record of the movement of the stars.

7) Calendars. They can measure the length of a year to three decimal points.

8) The Great Pyramid is an observatory for watching and recording the movements of the stars.

9) Centres of invisible forces of the Universe. Weird things can happen there – like blunt razors turning sharp and people feeling wobbly at the knees when they enter.

10) Maths calculators. Take the distance around the edges and the angles and whatnot and you can work out the distance round a circle (its circumference) if you know the distance across the diameter.

The biggest pyramid is the Pyramid of Cheops – known to this day as The Great Pyramid. How many times can you spot the word PYRAMID in the grid? The words may run across, up, down, diagonally, forwards or backwards.

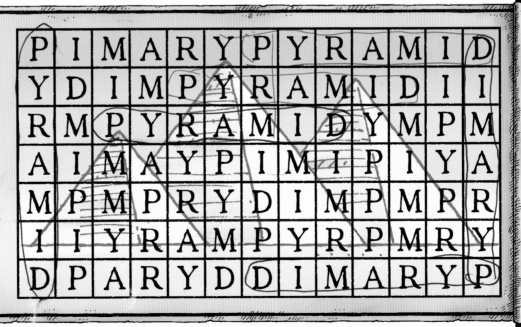

POTTY PYRAMIDS

Pyramids are H-U-G-E! The Great Pyramid in Giza is made up of about 2,300,000 stone blocks. If you broke the Great Pyramid into slabs 30cm thick, you could build a wall 1 metre high that would stretch all the way around France. If you had a little more time, you could cut the stone into rods about 6cm square – join them together and you'd have enough to reach the Moon!

Can you find the words listed in the pyramids? The words can be found written up, down, backwards and across. Then unscramble the letters in the mini pyramid to work out which civilization lived 5,000 years ago!

CAT
CHAMBER
CURSE
DESERT
EGYPT
EMBALM
GODS
GRAVE

MUMMY
NILE
PHARAOH
~~PRIEST~~
PYRAMID

ROBBER
SAND
SCRIBE
SPIRITS

SUN
TOMB
TREASURE

The – – – – – – – – –

I WOULDN'T BE SEEN DEAD IN ONE OF THOSE THINGS

DAILY BLAH
(7 January 1993)

STOP PRESS: News Flash

Archaeologists in Egypt have found the ruins of a small pyramid, a few metres from the Great Pyramid of Cheops at Giza. It was discovered by chance during a cleaning operation. This brings the number of known pyramids to 96. Can you count how many overlapping pyramids there are here?

Do you think you could be an artist? Here's your chance to prove yourself. A pharaoh has a new pyramid that needs to be decorated with the picture below. Copy the lines in each square onto the empty grid. Then colour your picture in.

Remember the Egyptian style. Heads are painted sideways, but the eye is shown full face. Legs are shown sideways and both shoulders should be in view. The more important the person, the bigger they are. Pharaoh gets most space.

If you work with some friends you could copy the drawing and make a wall painting. DANGER – don't use the living room wall without first asking … or you could be history.

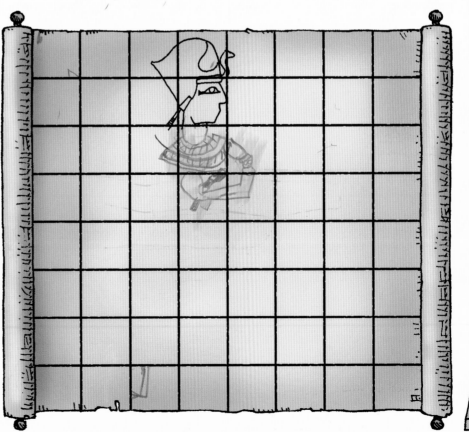

MAGICAL MUMMIES

Egyptians believed that one day the world would end. When it does, then everyone who has a body will move on to a wonderful afterlife. But if your body rots, you will miss out on this treat. So it was the Egyptians' duty to make sure their dead pharaohs didn't rot. They turned them into mummies.

The men who made dead bodies into mummies were called embalmers. They took the bodies to a place called the Beautiful House to work on them. Here's how to make a mummy. Unfortunately the instructions have been mixed up by a mummy's curse. Can you put them back in the right order?

A) Rip open the front of the body and take out the liver, the stomach, the intestines and the lungs – but leave the heart inside.

B) Throw the brain away and pack the skull with 'natron' – a sort of salt that stops bodies rotting.

C) Stuff the empty body with rags to give it the right shape, then sew it up.

D) Take the body to a Beautiful House – that's an open-ended tent in the open air – so the disgusting smells are blown away!

E) Wash the liver, the stomach, the intestines and the lungs in wine and place them in their sealed canopic jars.

F) Put the body on a wooden table with bars of wood (not a solid top) so you can reach underneath to bandage it.

G) Perform the ceremony of the 'Opening of the mouth' – or the mummy won't be able to eat, drink or speak in the next life!

H) Soak the body in natron for 70 days till it is well pickled.

I) Wrap the body in bandages from head to foot.

J) Remove the brain by pushing a chisel up the nose to break through, then hook the brain out with a piece of wire.

16

The following mummies will tell you a bit of mummy magic. Some of them are not telling the truth – can you work out which ones are?

IF A BIT FALLS OFF MY BODY, EMBALMERS WILL REPLACE IT WITH A LUMP OF WOOD

I WAS BURIED WITH A SCROLL OF MAGIC SPELLS CALLED 'THE BOOK OF THE DEAD'

THE LAST MUMMY WAS MADE IN 55BC

PEOPLE IN BRITAIN WATCHED MUMMIES BEING UNWRAPPED FOR FUN

MUMMIES MAKE GOOD FUEL FOR FIRE

EGYPTIANS BELIEVED THAT MUMMIES PASSED THROUGH A DANGEROUS PLACE FULL OF MONSTERS

BRITISH PEOPLE KEPT MUMMIES FOR DECORATION

7

Intestines can be pretty messy, so it's best to tidy them into a special container. The Egyptians made theirs out of clay. You can make one from a drinks bottle.

To make a canopic jar, you will need:
- An empty plastic drinks bottle
- Paints or felt-tip pens or pencils
- Modelling clay
- Drawing paper
- Sticky tape or glue
- Sand or pebbles

1) Take the top off the drinks bottle and rinse it out.
2) Put some sand or pebbles in the bottle to stop it falling over.
3) Decorate the paper with hieroglyphs and Egyptian pictures and symbols.

4) Wrap the paper round the bottle.
5) Tape or glue the paper to the bottle.

I THINK WE'LL NEED A BIGGER CANOPIC JAR

6) Use the modelling clay to make a lid. Make the lid into the shape of one of the four Sons of Horus.

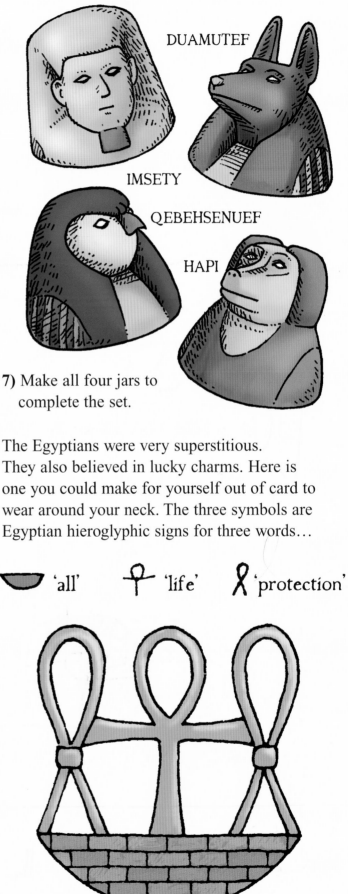

DUAMUTEF

IMSETY

QEBEHSENUEF

HAPI

7) Make all four jars to complete the set.

The Egyptians were very superstitious. They also believed in lucky charms. Here is one you could make for yourself out of card to wear around your neck. The three symbols are Egyptian hieroglyphic signs for three words…

'all'   'life'   'protection'

FATE OF THE MUMMY

After the pharaoh was turned into a mummy, they would be placed in a coffin in a tomb which was sealed. This was to shut out the grave-robbers. The dead person would then have to pass through a dangerous place known as the Duat. The dangers were monsters, boiling lakes and rivers of fire. The snake that spat poison was particularly nasty.

The monsters that live in the Duat could be overcome with the right spells. The spells were written down on Egyptian paper (papyrus) and left near the coffin. This is the 'Book of the Dead.' Can you help the dead pharaoh find his way through the Duat to the gates of Yaru (the Egyptian afterlife)?

At the gates of Yaru, the pharaoh's heart was placed in one side of a balance and in the other side was the Feather of Truth (this held all the lies of your past life). If the heart was lighter than the feather, the dead person was allowed through the gates. But if it was heavier … their heart was eaten by the Devourer. Colour in the dotted areas to find out what this terrifying monster looked like.

COULDN'T YOU GET A SMALLER FEATHER?

The Egyptians mummified more than their pharaohs. They mummified the pharaohs' pets and buried them in the pyramids to keep the dead kings company in the afterlife. Look at these two pictures. Spot ten differences between the two and circle them with a pencil.

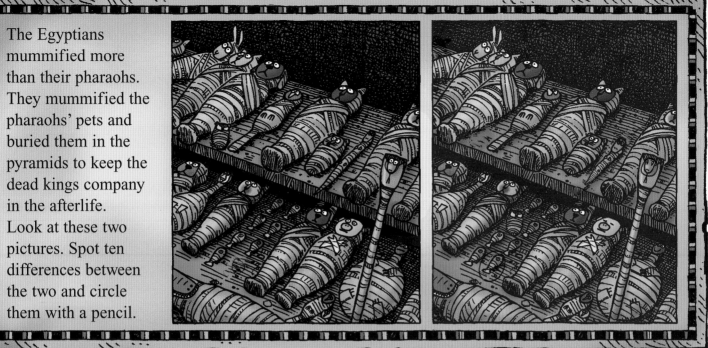

Pilgrims came to ancient Egypt like holiday-makers to Blackpool. They bought miniature mummies as souvenirs. To find out exactly what the Egyptians bought, answer all 5 questions below. Use your answers to work your way around the puzzle. You should only make words from letters that are next to each other. The letters that remain will give you the answer.

1) A magician pulls this long-eared creature out of a hat: rabbit (6)

2) When you're looking for a compliment you are said to be longing for one. (4)

3) Man's best friend: dog (3)

4) If your bedroom's in a mess, your mum would call it a pig sty! (3)

5) When you go under a very low bridge you should duck to avoid hitting your head. (4)

START

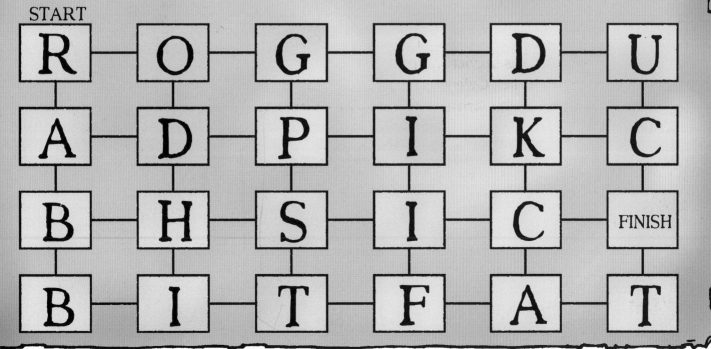

GRUESOME GRAVE-ROBBERS

Pyramids were filled with goodies so the pharaohs would be as rich in the next life as they were in this life. Of course they've all been robbed now – some were robbed at the time of the burial and the rest have been cleaned out by greedy treasure hunters in the twentieth century.

Pharaohs eventually realised that a pyramid was a huge stone advert saying, "Look at my grave! Look at my wealth!" The only answer was to hide the tombs. The pharaohs switched to being buried in hidden caves in the rocks. Help this grave-robber find the correct path that leads to the pharaoh's treasure.

START

FINISH

Cast yourself back in time a few thousand years. You are travelling through ancient Egypt and you've run out of copper coins. You want to rob a pyramid or a rock tomb (and get away with it). Answer Yes or No to the questions below and turn to page 24 to see if you have what it takes to become a successful grave-robber.

1) Do you do all the work yourself so that you get to keep all the loot?

2) Will you have to spend money to get people on your side?

3) Is it a good idea to go through the front entrance of the pyramid?

4) Should you bribe everyone concerned with the burial?

5) Is setting fire to the tomb a good idea?

6) As a grave-robber, should you avoid travelling merchants?

7) Should you spend your treasure so there's no evidence that it was you?

8) Is it easy to find your way around the inside of a pyramid?

9) Should you try to steal the body before it is buried?

10) Will you be punished if you get caught?

Many tomb-builders became grave-robbers. They grew hungry when their wages were late. They tried going on strike and marching on the officials' houses with chants of, "We are hungry! We are hungry!" When that failed they turned to robbing the tombs they'd helped to build. Look at the two scenes below. Spot eight differences between the two and circle them with a pencil.

CURIOUS CURSES

Mummies are a bit creepy. Looking at corpses of long-dead people is enough to give you goose-bumps on your goose-bumps! But it's not creepy enough for some people. They imagine the mummies aren't just shrivelled flesh — they believe the mummy spirits wander around. These spirits bring curses and spells to the living people who disturb their rest and rob their graves.

Lots of 'true' mummy stories have been told over the past century. This is one of them — see if you believe it! Count Louis Hamon wrote to his friend, Lord Carnarvon. He begged him to be careful on his expedition in Egypt. Put the pictures in the right order to find out why Louis Hamon wanted to warn his friend.

G 1375 BC... KING AKHNATON ARGUED WITH HIS DAUGHTER
TAKE HER AWAY... EXECUTE HER!

C THEN LOCK IT IN THE SAFE AND LET'S FORGET ABOUT IT...

J A SUDDEN WIND TORE OPEN THE DOOR... THE HAMONS FELL TO THE FLOOR AND AN EGYPTIAN WOMAN APPEARED

I HAMON'S WIFE HATED IT ON SIGHT...
CAN'T YOU GIVE IT TO A MUSEUM?
I'VE TRIED — THEY ALL REFUSE

D BUT AS HE CLOSED THE BOOK, THE HOUSE WAS PLUNGED INTO DARKNESS... A BLAST SHOOK THE HOUSE

F BUT IN OCTOBER 1922 THE HAMONS OPENED THE SAFE. THEY STOOD BACK IN HORROR...
IT'S NOT MUMMIFIED. IT'S AS SOFT AND FRESH AS MINE

E THE HAND
GONE!

L DESTROY IT!
NO, SHE DESERVES A DECENT FUNERAL

N AND ON 31 OCTOBER, HALLOWE'EN, HAMON READ PRAYERS FROM AN ANCIENT "BOOK OF THE DEAD"

A BUT HE WASN'T SATISFIED WITH HER DEATH
CUT OFF HER HAND! WITHOUT A COMPLETE BODY SHE WILL NOT ENTER THE AFTERLIFE

H THE GRISLY RELIC, THE HAND, WAS PASSED DOWN THROUGH ARAB FAMILIES, TILL THIS CENTURY, IT REACHED A SHEIK
YOU HAVE CURED ME OF MALARIA, HAMON, LET ME GIVE YOU A GIFT

B AND THE SHEIK GAVE HAMON THE PRINCESS'S HAND
I COULDN'T ACCEPT SUCH A... A PRECIOUS GIFT...
I INSIST!

O THE FIGURE BENT OVER THE HAND AND VANISHED

M SO THE PRINCESS WAS BURIED... BUT HER HAND WAS NOT

K LOOK! SHE HAS NO HAND!

Fill in the grid below with the correct sequence.

| G | | | | | | C | | | | | | |

Lord Carnarvon ignored his friend's letter. His expedition found the fabulous tomb of Tutankhamun and seven weeks after that, Lord Carnarvon was dead! He got a mosquito bite on his left cheek which became infected. When doctors examined Tutankhamun's mummy, they noticed a strange mark – on his left cheek! Copy the picture boxes into the grid to see the full picture.

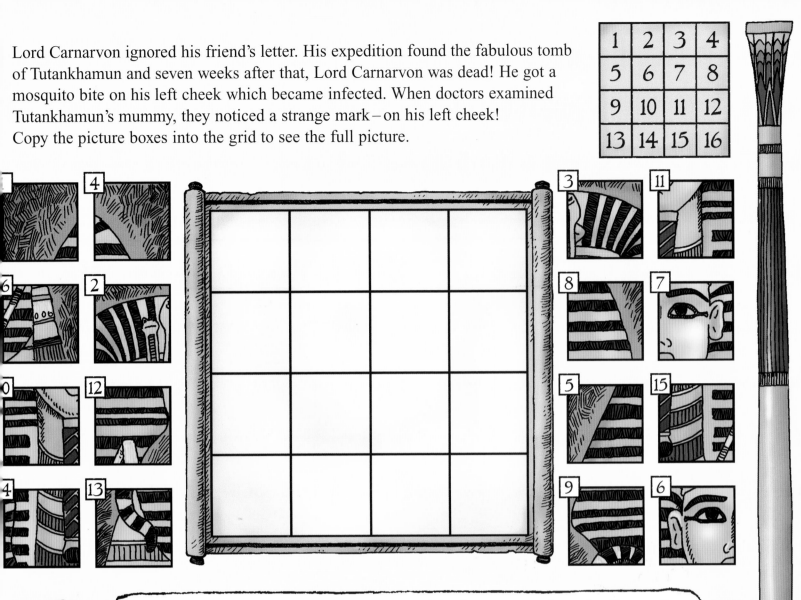

The death of Lord Carnarvon was one of the first stories about the Curse of Tutankhamun's Tomb. Each of the following six stories has been told by someone at some time. Can you work out which stories are simply LIES, which are MISTAKES and which are TRUE but can be explained?

1) Arthur Mace was one of the first to enter the tomb and he died shortly after.

2) When Tutankhamun's mummy was unwrapped, the archaeologists found a curse wrapped in the bandages. It said: 'They who enter this sacred tomb shall swiftly be visited by the wings of death.'

3) When Lord Carnarvon died, his favourite dog howled and died at the exact moment of his death. The dog was 3,000 miles away in England.

4) A worker in the British Museum was fastening labels to things stolen from Tutankhamun's tomb. He dropped dead shortly after.

5) American millionaire George Gould visited the tomb. He was fine before he went, but died the next day.

6) The mummy's 'curse' is in fact ancient Egyptian germs that were sealed into the tomb 3,000 years ago.

WHO WERE THE GROOVY GREEKS?

The groovy Greeks hung out over 2,000 years ago, from 1600 BC to AD 146, when the rotten Romans took over. These hip 'n' happening Greeks were a mixed bunch – there were horrible heroes, savage Spartans, phoolish philosophers, suffering slaves and ingenious inventors. Their influence is still with us today.

Here's a quick quiz to see how much you know about the groovy Greeks. Simply answer 'Yea' for yes or 'Nay' for no.

1) A slave called Aesop told great stories such as 'The Tortoise and the Hare'. He was richly rewarded by the Greek priests.
2) In the story of Troy, King Agamemnon sacrifices his daughter to the gods. Would that have really happened in ancient Greece?
3) The Greeks read the future using dead birds.

WHAT!.. NO DOG FOOD!

WHAT DO THEY SAY?

IN THE FUTURE THERE WILL BE FEWER BIRDS

4) Hecate was the Greek goddess of crossroads. She would appear with ghosts and phantom dogs. The Greeks left food at crossroads for her.
5) The children who lived in the city of Sparta were super-tough kids. One Spartan boy hid a stolen fox cub under his tunic and didn't let on, even though the fox ate the boy's guts away.

The Greeks were very groovy with numbers. Polybius, born in 200 BC, was a Greek historian of Rome. He is famous for a series of history books that contained 40 volumes, but he also had time to invent this code, now known as Polybius' Checkerboard. Each letter has a pair of numbers – the horizontal (across) number followed by the vertical (up-down). So B is 1-2, but F is 2-1. The word 'Yes' is 54 15 43.

Use the checkerboard to work this out…

44 15 11 13 23 15 42 43   14 34 33'44
25 33 34 52   15 51 15 42 54 44 23 24 33 22
44 23 15 54   24 45 43 44   44 42 54   44 34
25 24 14   54 34 45   44 23 11 44
44 23 15 54   14 34

31 11 44 15   11 22 11 24 33   12 34 54

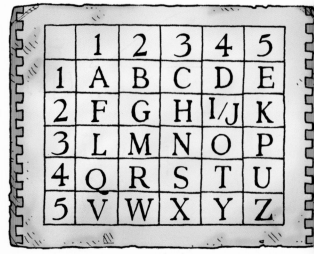

	1	2	3	4	5
1	A	B	C	D	E
2	F	G	H	I/J	K
3	L	M	N	O	P
4	Q	R	S	T	U
5	V	W	X	Y	Z

The Greeks also invented other groovy devices which are still important to us today. One of the cleverest was the camera obscura – or the 'pinhole' camera. A Greek artist covered a window with a dark material, then punched a small hole through. An upside-down image of the scene was seen on the inside wall and traced by the artist. You could have a go at making your own, slightly smaller version.

1) Make a box of black card, 20 x 10 x 10 cm.

2) Make a small pinhole in black paper at one end.

3) Place grease-proof paper across the other end.

4) Hold it up to a bright scene.

5) The scene will be 'projected' on to the grease-proof paper.

Note: this image will be upside-down – you may have to stand on your head to get the best view!

BACK

20cm

FRONT

GREASE-PROOF PAPER

BLACK PAPER

BLACK BOX

PINHOLE

The Greeks invented some crazy customs for weddings and funerals. Match the right customs to the right events and answer: a wedding, a funeral or both.

1) YOU SHOULD SACRIFICE A LUMP OF YOUR HAIR TO THE GODS BEFORE...
2) YOU SHOULD SHUT THE EYES AND THE MOUTH OF THE MAIN PERSON AT...
3) YOU SHOULD HAVE A TORCH–LIT PROCESSION AT...
4) YOU SHOULD BEAT YOUR HEAD AND TEAR YOUR HAIR AT...
5) YOU SHOULD GIVE THE MAIN PERSON A BATH BEFORE...
6) YOU SHOULD SING AND DANCE AT...
7) YOU SHOULD PLACE A CROWN ON THE HEAD OF THE MAIN PERSON AT...
8) YOU SHOULD THROW FRUIT AND NUTS...
9) YOU SHOULD GIVE GIFTS OF POTTERY, STONE VASES AND MIRRORS AT...
10) YOU SHOULD LEAVE THE PARTY EARLY IF YOU ARE A WOMAN AT...

GRUESOME GODS

The Greeks loved stories, especially horror stories. What about Cronos, chief of the gods? This gruesome god ate his own children. Then eleven babies later, he gave a heavenly heave and threw them all up! The young gods grew to overthrow their dreadful dad. So it was goodbye Cronos – hello Zeus and company.

These new gods were just one big, unhappy family. They were always fighting, arguing and doing horrible things to each other. Can you untangle the names and match the description to each god?

A

B

C

1) SUEZ
Of all the groovy gods, this one was the grooviest. When he wasn't flirting with women, he was frying someone with a thunderbolt.

2) POISONED
Brother to the top god. This sore loser ruled the sea. He stomped around, whipping up the seas with a fork and creating storms. What a stirrer!

3) SHADE
Second brother of the top god and a real loser.
He won the job of ruling the underworld. That must have been hell!

4) A HIRED POT
This lady was the goddess of love and beauty.

5) LOO PAL
This was the sun god and also the god of prophecy.

6) A THANE
The goddess of wisdom and war. What a combination.

D

E

F

The Greek myths are still popular today – in story books, on television and even at the cinema. They tell of murder, revenge, suffering and lots of death. Test your knowledge and match the sentences below.

1) Paris judged a goddess beauty competition and …

2) Icarus flew too close to the sun and …

3) Cerberus, the three-headed dog …

4) Anyone who looked at Medusa, an ugly snake-haired gorgon …

5 Mighty Atlas became so arrogant that he …

6) When Pandora opened the box she …

a) let out greed and envy, hatred and cruelty, poverty and hunger, sickness and despair.

b) was doomed to stand forever, bearing the weight of the world.

c) guarded the entrance to Hades, or hell.

d) melted the wax on his wings.

e) turned to stone.

f) gave the winner a golden apple.

FIGHT LIKE A GREEK

Groovy Greeks loved stories about heroes – men who were almost as powerful as gods. There was a snag … they were mortal and so could die. Stories about heroes were told as poems and sung in the ancient palaces of Greece. Later, they were written down. The oldest poem was by the writer Homer, who wrote an epic poem called The Iliad, all about the siege of Troy. Heroes fought to the death to get the most beautiful woman in the world, Helen, back to hubby, King Menelaus.

Everyone knows the story of the wooden horse of Troy. But can you believe it? Put these pictures in the correct order to read what happened when those Trojan twits saw a wooden horse standing outside the gates of the city.

Correct order of pictures:

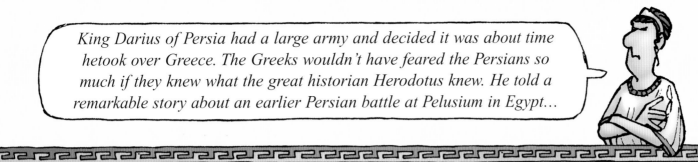

King Darius of Persia had a large army and decided it was about time he took over Greece. The Greeks wouldn't have feared the Persians so much if they knew what the great historian Herodotus knew. He told a remarkable story about an earlier Persian battle at Pelusium in Egypt…

On the battlefield I saw a strange thing which the natives pointed out to me. The bones of the dead lay scattered on the field in two lots – those of the Persians and those of the Egyptians. If, then, you strike a Persian skull, they are so weak you will break a hole in them. But the Egyptian skulls are so strong that you may hit them with a rock and hardly crack them.

Count how many Persian and Egyptian skulls you can see in this picture to see who won.

Can you work out which of these things were first seen in ancient Greece.

1) SOAP
2) CAMERA
3) PARACHUTE
4) ANCHOR
5) CHEWING GUM
6) SIREN
7) CATAPULT
8) SANDWICHES
9) ROLLER SKATES
10) SPECTACLES

29

SAVAGE SPARTANS

The Spartans were the toughest of all the Greeks.
They believed they were better than anyone else. If they wanted more
land then they just moved into someone else's patch. If someone was
already living there the Spartans just made them slaves. In short,
they were the ungrooviest lot in the whole of Greece.

Life was extra-tough for Spartan kids. Add the missing words to
read these strict Spartan rules.

MISSING WORDS NOT IN THE CORRECT ORDER: mountains, hair, herd, bite, baths, no clothes, beaten.

1) A child belongs to the state of Sparta. At the age of seven, children will join a _____.

2) A bad serving-child will receive a _____ on the back of the hand.

3) A sickly baby will be taken to the _____.

4) A new bride must cut off her _____ and dress like a man.

5) Children caught stealing food will be _____.

6) A Spartan child may have only a few _____ a year.

7) In processions, dances and temple services, girls must wear _____.

THAT THASOS IS A CLEANLINESS FREAK

YEAH... THAT'S HIS THIRD BATH THIS YEAR

One Spartan general wanted to betray his country. But things didn't quite go
to plan. Unscramble the words in CAPITAL LETTERS to read the story.
The number in brackets tells you where the words should go in the grid.
The blue column will tell you the name of this sly Spartan.

One great Spartan general helped to FATEED (2) the Persians in 479 BC. But the Spartans thought he was getting too big-headed. He was asked to return to STARAP (1) to be UPDISHEN (3). The general was not happy. He wrote to the Persian NIKG (6), Xerxes, and offered to betray Sparta. The nosy messenger opened the letter to find a deadly 'Ps – LIKL (7) the messenger!' So, the messenger took it back to Sparta, and they sent a force to kill the RATTIOR (5). The general fled to a temple in Athena, but the SISNSASAS (4) bricked up the door and starved him to death. Later, the general's THOGS (9) came back to THUNA (8) the temple. In the end, the priestess sent for a magician – a sort of groovy Greek ghostbuster – to get rid of him.

1 S T A R A P
2 F A T E E D
3 U P D I S H E N
4 S I S N S A S A S
5 R A T T I O R
6 N I K G
7 L I K L
8 T H U N A
9 T H O G S

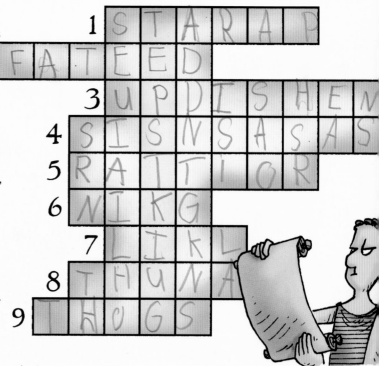

30

Spartans lied, cheated and tricked their way out of trouble. If this didn't work, they died fighting. King Leonidas led 300 Spartans to defend Thermopylae against tens of thousands of Persians. The Persian leader, Xerxes, couldn't believe the Spartans would be daft enough to fight and die. Xerxes didn't know the Spartans. Look at the two battle scenes below. Spot ten differences between the two and circle them with a pencil.

LIVE LIKE A GREEK

Athens, being really groovy, had the first democracy. This is a society where every adult has a vote on laws and how money is spent. But because the Greeks still had a lot to learn, they didn't quite get it right! Everyone had the vote except women, poor people, anyone under 30 years and slaves. So, ancient Greece wasn't as perfect as they liked to think.

Being a female in ancient Greece wasn't much fun. They were told what to do and what not to do – they didn't have the freedom that the men enjoyed (those that weren't slaves that is). Which of the following statements are true and which are false?

1) A WOMAN MAY BUY OR SELL ANYTHING THAT IS WORTH MORE THAN A SMALL MEASURE OF BARLEY.

2) A WOMAN MUST LEARN TO SPIN, WEAVE, COOK AND MANAGE SLAVES.

3) A WOMAN MUST WORSHIP THE GODDESS HESTIA.

4) A WOMAN MUST BE BROUGHT UP WITH SLAVES AND LEARN HOUSEHOLD SKILLS.

5) A WOMAN MUST STAY AT HOME.

6) A WOMAN MAY OWN THINGS OTHER THAN HER CLOTHES, JEWELLERY AND SLAVES.

7) A WOMAN OUGHT TO HAVE A HUSBAND (CHOSEN BY HER FATHER) WHEN SHE IS 15.

8) A WOMAN MUST NOT GO OUT EXCEPT TO VISIT OTHER WOMEN OR TO GO TO RELIGIOUS FESTIVALS, WEDDINGS AND FUNERALS.

9) A WOMAN MAY ALLOW ANYONE TO VISIT WITHOUT HER HUSBAND KNOWING.

10) A WOMAN MAY VOTE.

FEMALE? FEMALE? NO FEMALES HERE! JUST US BLOKES

Life was even worse for slaves. Alexandria was a city in Egypt ruled by the Greeks. Around 250 BC they had a set of rules which help us to understand how Greek law worked. Can you match the crime to the punishment?

1) A free man strikes another free man or free woman.

2) A slave strikes a free man or free woman.

3) A drunk person injures someone else.

4) A free man threatens another with wood, iron or bronze.

5) A slave threatens another with wood, iron or bronze.

a) Fine of 100 drachmas.

b) Fine of 200 drachmas.

c) A hundred lashes.

d) A hundred lashes.

e) Fine of 100 drachmas.

From 500–200 BC, the Greeks had a ruthless way of treating babies. Follow the steps below to see if you would have made a good parent in ancient Greece.

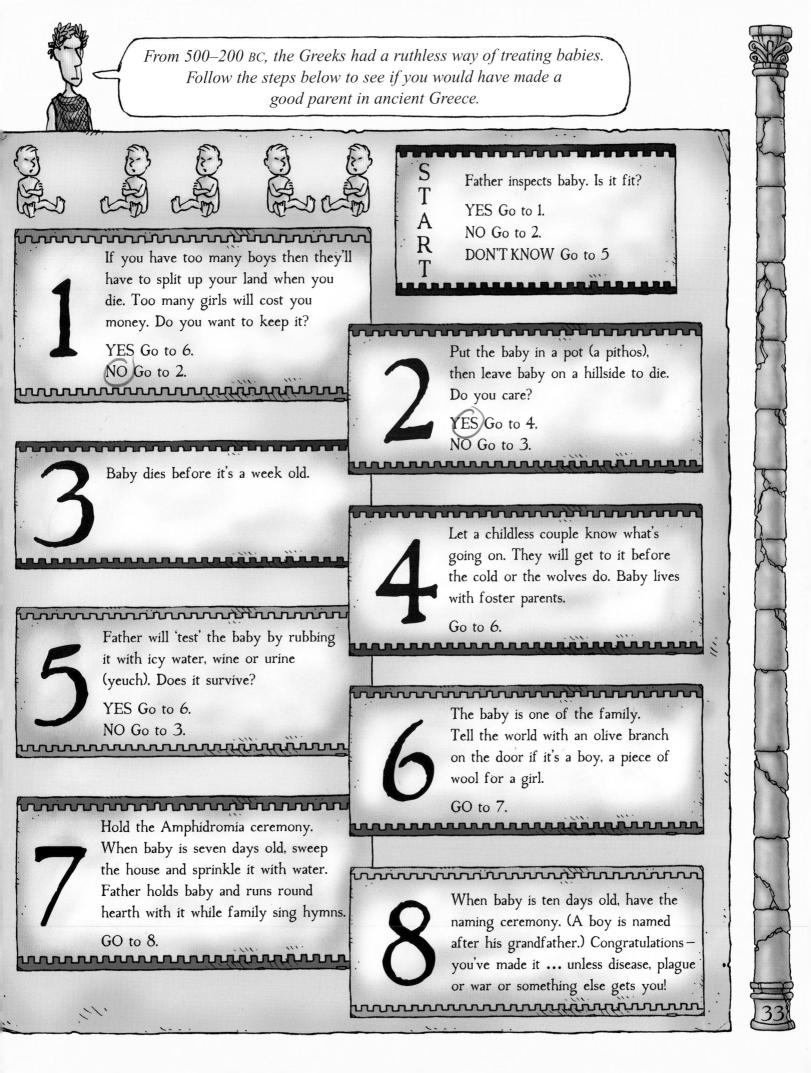

START

Father inspects baby. Is it fit?

YES Go to 1.
NO Go to 2.
DON'T KNOW Go to 5

1

If you have too many boys then they'll have to split up your land when you die. Too many girls will cost you money. Do you want to keep it?

YES Go to 6.
NO Go to 2.

2

Put the baby in a pot (a pithos), then leave baby on a hillside to die. Do you care?

YES Go to 4.
NO Go to 3.

3

Baby dies before it's a week old.

4

Let a childless couple know what's going on. They will get to it before the cold or the wolves do. Baby lives with foster parents.

Go to 6.

5

Father will 'test' the baby by rubbing it with icy water, wine or urine (yeuch). Does it survive?

YES Go to 6.
NO Go to 3.

6

The baby is one of the family. Tell the world with an olive branch on the door if it's a boy, a piece of wool for a girl.

GO to 7.

7

Hold the Amphidromia ceremony. When baby is seven days old, sweep the house and sprinkle it with water. Father holds baby and runs round hearth with it while family sing hymns.

GO to 8.

8

When baby is ten days old, have the naming ceremony. (A boy is named after his grandfather.) Congratulations — you've made it ... unless disease, plague or war or something else gets you!

GROOVY GREEK GAMES

The Groovy Greeks liked nothing better than a contest. The first Olympic games were simple foot races, around 776 BC. The first few Olympics had just one race on one day – a race of about 190 metres or the length of the stadium. Other longer races were added over the years until the meeting lasted five days. There was even a junior Olympics for kids!

Here's a quick quiz to see how much you know about the groovy Olympics. Simply answer 'Yea' for yes or 'Nay' for no.

1) When the winners got home they were given free haircuts as extra rewards.

2) At the first Olympic games the winner was given a cauldron as a prize.

3) A wreath made from parsley leaves was given as a prize.

4) Mule racing was one of the sports at the Olympics.

5) The sport of 'pancration' was a mix of boxing and wrestling where you could jump on your opponent.

6) Sometimes a winner cheated by paying the judges. If he was caught the winner could lose the title.

7) The Greeks had their own names for their contests. One of the games was called hoplitodromos.

8) The spoilsport Romans came along and banned the Olympics in AD 394.

Can you find these words listed in the puzzle? The words can be found written forwards or backwards. Then unscramble the letters that are left to work out the name of the goddess of victory, who watched over all athletic contests.

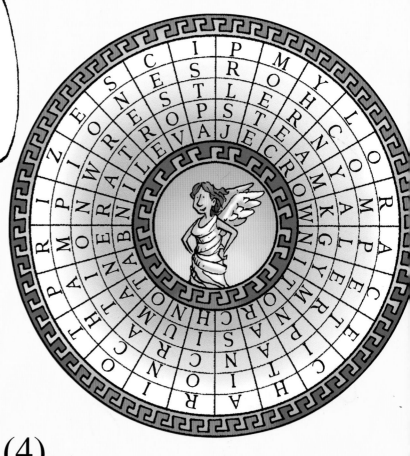

ARENA, BATON, CHAMPION, CHARIOT, COMPETITION, CROWN, GYMNASIUM, HORSE, JAVELIN, OLYMPICS, PANCRATION, PRIZE, RACE, RELAY, SPORT, TEAM, TORCH, WRESTLER

GODDESS _ _ _ _ (4)

1. Champion wrestler, Timanthese, lost his strength. He was so upset he did what?
   a) He built a tower and threw himself off the top.
   b) He built a fire and threw himself into it.
   c) He built a pond and drowned himself in it.

I'M NOT TAKING ANY CHANCES

2. Handsome Creugas and big bully Damoxenos fought to a standstill in a boxing match. The referee said they could each have one free shot at the other. Damoxenos killed Creugas with a cheat. What did he do?
   a) He pulled a knife out of his hair band and stabbed Creugas.
   b) He borrowed a nearby javelin and speared Creugas.
   c) He used his sharp fingernails to rip Creugas's belly open and then pulled out his guts.

I'M GUTTED!

3. The Olympics were supposed to have started when King Oeomaus said to young Pelops, 'You want to marry my daughter? Then race me in a chariot.' Pelops won when King Oeomaus died. How?
   a) Pelops nobbled Oeomaus's chariot.
   b) Pelops nobbled Oeomaus's horses.
   c) Pelops nobbled Oeomaus's drink.

4. Wrestler Milo won five Olympic games as a wrestler and was super-strong. (He once held up the collapsing roof of a building while people escaped.) But he died when he tried his strength against what?
   a) a lion
   b) a tree
   c) a woman

TICKLE TICKLE TICKLE

5. Wrestler Polydamas was another super-strong man. He once held a fierce bull so firmly it had to tear its own hoof off to escape. (Yeuch!) How did his strength finish him off?
   a) He tried to copy Milo by holding up a collapsing roof.
   b) He tried to copy Greek god Heracles by fighting a lion with his bare hands.
   c) He tried to copy his old trick of ripping off a bull's hoof.

EVEN GROOVIER GREEK GAMES

You didn't have to be an athlete to enjoy games. Greek children invented games that are still played in some parts of the world today. In fact, you may have played some of the games yourself. If you haven't, and want to play like a groovy Greek, then here are some of the best.

The Greeks played ball games where you throw a ball at a 'wicket', rather like cricket without a batsman. We have pictures of these games that have been painted on Greek vases, but we don't have their rules. Maybe they played like this...

Greecket

1) Stand on a mark a fixed distance from the wicket.
2) Take a ball and have ten attempts to hit the wicket.
3) Your opponent stands behind the wicket (like a wicket-keeper) and throws the ball back to you every time.
4) Then you stand behind the wicket while your opponent tries.
5) The one who has the most hits on the wicket from ten throws is the winner. It looks (from the vase paintings) as if the loser has to give the winner a piggy-back ride!

> WHY IS IT ALWAYS THE BIG KIDS WHO ARE GOOD AT GAMES?

Bronze Fly

This game is a sort of Greek Blind-man's Buff. A Greek described it...

> THEY FASTENED A HEADBAND ROUND A BOY'S EYES. HE TURNED ROUND AND ROUND AND CALLED OUT, 'I WILL CHASE THE BRONZE FLY!' THE OTHERS CALLED BACK, 'YOU MIGHT CHASE HIM BUT YOU WON'T CATCH HIM.' THEY THEN TORMENT HIM WITH PAPER WHIPS UNTIL HE CATCHES ONE OF THEM.

> ISN'T THAT A BULL WHIP?

> NOT VERY GOOD ARE YOU?

Kottabos

To play this game, you will need a cup of water and a 50p coin on the end of a broom handle. Even grown-up Greeks played this silly game with wine at parties.
1) Take a broom handle and stand it upright.
2) Balance a 50p on top of the pole.
3) Grip the cup of water by the handle.
4) Flick the water out and try to knock the coin off the top of the pole.

HORRIBLE HISTORIES

HORRIBLE HISTORIES

In the game called Ephedrismos, a player was blindfolded and gave someone a piggy-back. The rider had to guide the player to a target. This would have been a competition where pairs of players raced to reach the target. Can you work out which path will lead the players to the target?

START

FINISH

DIE LIKE A GREEK

The first Greek doctors didn't work from a hospital, they worked from a temple. The temple was famous because no one ever died there. The doctor-priests cheated. If someone was dying when they arrived then they weren't allowed in. And if they started dying once they got inside, they were dumped in the nearby woods.

Hippocrates was a Greek doctor who believed in the proper study of the body using experiments. Hippocrates also had advice for doctors. He obviously took it – he lived until he was 99! Read the text, then find the words in CAPITALS in the wordsearch. The words are written forwards, backwards, up, down, diagonally and across.

Hippo took samples from his patients and tested them. But he couldn't test them in a laboratory with chemicals the way modern doctors can. He tested them by tasting them or making his patient taste them. Which of the following horrible things were tasted to test? Answer 'Yummy yes' or 'Nasty no'.

A DOCTOR must be careful not to get too FAT. Someone who can't look after his own FITNESS shouldn't be allowed to look after other people's. Secondly, he should be CLEAN, wear good CLOTHES and use a sweet (but not too strong) SCENT. This is pleasant when visiting the SICK. He must not look too grim or too cheerful – a GRIM man will worry the PATIENT while a laughing man may be seen as an IDIOT.

A	O	C	S	S	E	N	T	I	F
H	I	C	L	O	T	H	E	S	O
O	A	R	D	E	I	O	C	P	R
I	D	I	O	T	A	I	D	A	G
R	F	A	N	P	Q	N	S	T	C
O	M	I	R	G	L	T	R	I	S
T	A	P	A	T	E	N	O	E	K
C	F	O	S	N	L	E	P	N	C
O	L	T	T	D	O	C	R	T	I
D	B	T	A	F	E	S	S	A	S

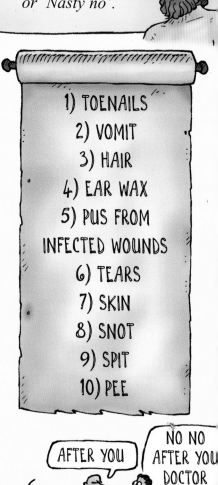

1) TOENAILS
2) VOMIT
3) HAIR
4) EAR WAX
5) PUS FROM INFECTED WOUNDS
6) TEARS
7) SKIN
8) SNOT
9) SPIT
10) PEE

AFTER YOU

NO NO AFTER YOU DOCTOR

Not every doctor was as good as Hippocrates. King Pyrrhus of Greece had a deadly doctor in 278 BC. The doc wrote to the Romans and said he was willing to poison the Greek king if they paid him. But the Romans sent the letter straight back to Pyrrhus to tell him there was a traitor in his camp – they didn't want to be blamed for the murder. Can you lead the messenger back to the Greek camp before the doctor does the deadly deed?

39

FUNNY FOOD

One historian said, 'The Greeks had meals of two courses; the first a kind of porridge – and the second a kind of porridge.' It wasn't quite that bad. You'd find much more at a groovy Greek meal. Peasants liked olives, figs, nuts or goat's milk cheese. As time went by, the diet got richer, and the rich started to eat more and more meat. Roast goat was a particular favourite.

A sacrifice is supposed to be a groovy gift to the gods. When the Greeks sacrificed an animal to a god, they roasted it and they ate it. That's a bit like buying your mum a box of chocolates then scoffing them yourself. Answer the questions below to find out more about the Greek's gruesome eating habits.

1. At a sacrifice, the greatest honour was to eat:
a) roasted heart, lungs, liver or kidney
b) the tail
c) the chargilled eyeballs

2. What did the Greeks leave behind for the gods?
a) tail, thigh bones and gall bladder
b) nothing
c) skin

3. Greeks mixed the blood and fat together and stuffed it into the bladder of an animal. People these days ask for this at the butchers – what is it?
a) haggis
b) black pudding
c) sausage

DON'T YOU THINK YOU'RE TAKING THE SACRIFICE THING A LITTLE TOO FAR?

4. There was no sugar in those days. How did the ancient Greeks sweeten their food?
a) crushed grapes
b) herbs
c) honey

5. Vegetarians in ancient Greece sacrificed:
a) vegetables
b) cows that had died of old age
c) sticks

SHE'S TORTURING THAT BRUSSEL SPROUT!

GOOD

6. The Spartans had a disgusting concoction called Black Broth. It was made from:
a) fish guts
b) mixed pork juices, salt and vinegar
c) calf's feets and vegetables

7. Aristotle, the great Greek teacher, had a favourite meat. What was it?
a) camel
b) turkey
c) horse liver

ONE HUMP OR TWO?

After about 500 BC, the rich started to eat meat – goat, mutton, pork and deer. But they also had a taste for some unusual food. Unscramble the words to read what food is on the menu. Then decide which foods the ancient Greeks would and wouldn't have eaten.

WHAT A PIG!

1) SHE HURTS

2) DEEP FROGS IV

3) SAUCER SHIN

4) ODDER HIKING SYRUP

5) SOCK CAGE PEG

6) YAK SCENE HO

7) SPURN IT

8) OWLES FEEREDS

9) PERHAPS GROSS

10) TIGHT PEAS

Milon was a wrestler. He was also a very greedy Greek. Read the story below. Then find the words in CAPITALS in the wordsearch. The words are written forwards, backwards, up, down and diagonally.

Milon thought he was pretty groovy. Before one OLYMPIC contest he walked around a STADIUM with a live young BULL on his SHOULDERS. Then, he KILLED the bull and ate it. He finished the whole bull before the day was out. The GODS decided to teach him a LESSON. It happened when Milon was showing off again. He SPLIT open a tree with his hands ... but they became stuck in the split. Try as he might he couldn't get free. When a pack of WOLVES came along they licked their chops and moved in on Milon. What do you think they did to Milon? Just what Milon did to the young bull – except they probably didn't COOK him first.

NIBBLE NIBBLE NIBBLE

S	D	E	L	L	I	K	O	C
R	D	H	A	E	L	O	L	H
E	C	O	O	S	I	O	Y	O
D	U	H	G	S	K	C	M	S
L	S	C	A	O	R	Y	P	E
U	I	P	F	N	S	T	I	V
O	D	K	L	P	D	Q	C	L
H	T	L	O	I	Y	S	G	O
S	U	H	T	O	T	W	I	W
B	C	M	U	I	D	A	T	S

THINK LIKE A GREEK

The Greeks had some of the cleverest thinkers of ancient times. Yet they had some very strange beliefs. They were very superstitious and believed in horoscopes, ghosts and gods deciding their fate. They believed that the gods spoke through 'Oracles', a priest or priestess, and you could learn about the future…

At the Corinth Oracle, you could speak directly to a god. You spoke to the alter … and a voice boomed back. Visitors believed it was a miracle. The truth is, a secret tunnel led under the alter. A priest crawled through the tunnel. He listened to the speaker and answered through a tube. Can you find your way through this maze to the cheating priest?

People today are nervous about walking under a ladder because they think it will bring them bad luck, or they touch wood to bring them good luck. The Greeks had their own strange superstitions. Fill in the missing words to read about what they believed…

Missing words not in the correct order: messengers, wickedness, earth, moon, spirits, protected, evil, bodies, dead, disease, tar, reflection, die

1) Birds were <u>spirits</u> between <u>earth</u> and heaven, and the <u>moon</u> was a resting place for spirits on their way to heaven.

2) Some Greeks kept dead <u>bodies</u> in jars called pithos. But sometimes, they said, the spirits of th_____ escaped from the jars and began to bother the living with illness and _____. The best way to stop the wicked spirits from getting into your house was to paint _____ round the door frames.

3) The Greeks believed that if you dreamed about seeing your _____ in a mirror then you would _____ soon after.

4) Greeks thought there were _____ called 'daimons' around. Some were good and _____ you; some were _____ and could lead you into _____.

I WISH THEY' SEND SHOR° MESSAG°

IT WASN'T ME SIR, IT WAS MY DAIMON

Can you imagine your maths teacher setting up his own religion? This is what the famous teacher, Pythagoras, did. He and his followers lived apart from the rest of the Greek people and had some rather strange beliefs. Read these ridiculous rules and decide which ones are true and which ones are false.

1) DON'T EAT BEANS.

2) DON'T EAT THE HEART OF AN ANIMAL.

3) DON'T LOOK IN A MIRROR BESIDE A LAMP.

4) DON'T WALK ALONG THE MAIN STREET.

5) DON'T TOUCH A WHITE COCKEREL.

ALL I DID WAS ASK HIM TO HELP ME MOVE THESE WHITE COCKERELS

6) DON'T STAND ON YOUR FINGERNAIL CLIPPINGS.

How many of the following facts can you rearrange into the right order.

1) The Greek explorer, Pytheas,	ran about naked in the woods	his dead mother's coffin
2) The Greek teacher, Gorgias,	trained in	hockey
3) Spartan youths	cut off a girl's head	on the statues of Greek gods
4) A Greek sportsman	was born in	the North Sea
5) The girls of Attica	enjoyed the team sport called	you shouldn't touch a fire with an iron poker
6) The Greek teacher, Pythagoras,	believed	pretending to be bears
7) The Greek doctor, Aesculapius,	knocked off the naughty bits	to cure water on the brain
8) General Alcibiades	sailed to	the secret police

MEET THE LEGENDARY INCA LORDS

Around AD 1250, in an area we now call Peru in South America, tribes of people began to appear in the Andes mountains. To begin with, there were many different tribes, but the Incas defeated them all. Legend says that over a period of time, eight different Inca lords ruled over Cuzco – the Inca's valley.

Put the six pictures below in the correct order, to find out how the first lord, Manco Capac, discovered Cuzco.

C

THE INCAS STARTED TO LOOK FOR GOOD SOIL TO FARM AND GROW CROPS IN. THEN MANCO HAD A BRIGHT IDEA...

MY BROTHERS EAT TOO MUCH! THERE'LL BE MORE FOOD FOR THE REST OF US IF I KILL THEM!

F

AT LAST THE INCAS ARRIVED AT CUZCO

SEEMS LIKE A NICE PLACE

A

THERE WERE PEOPLE LIVING THERE ALREADY. NO PROBLEM.

PUSH OFF PEASANTS! THIS IS INCA LAND NOW!

BOOT

D

THE INCAS SETTLED THERE AND INTRODUCED THEMSELVES TO THE NEW NEIGHBOURS

WE'RE THE INCAS. PAY US OR WE'LL KILL YOU.

B

IN TIME THEY HAD CHILDREN...

LET'S CALL THIS LITTLE CHAP SINCHI ROCA

E

THAT'S WHAT HE DID. ONE WAS SEALED IN A CAVE AND TWO WERE TURNED TO STONE. THEN HE DID SOMETHING VERY STRANGE...

I NEED A WIFE. I CAN'T MARRY ONE OF THE COMMON PEOPLE. I'LL MARRY MY SISTER, MAMA OCLLO!

HELP!

CORRECT ORDER OF PICTURES... | C | | | | | |

Can you match the questions with the correct lord?

1st Lord: Manco Capac

2nd Lord: Sinchi Roca

3rd Lord: Lloque Yupanqui

4th Lord: Mayta Capac

5th Lord: Capac Yupanqui

6th Lord: Inca Roca

7th Lord: Yahuar Huacac

8th Lord: Viracocha

1) Which lord's clever mama tricked everyone into thinking her son was the new ruler sent by the Sun God?

2) Which vile lord called himself 'Creator God'?

3) Which lord was as big as an eight-year-old by his first birthday?

4) Which lord had more than one wife, which proved to have deadly consequences for his second son?

5) Which lord won the heart of the lovely Mama Mikay and made a sworn enemy of the Ayarmaca leader in the process?

6) Which lord was named ruler because his elder brother was too ugly to rule?

7) Which lord was so ugly that people who saw him ran away?

8) Which lord first saw the light of day when he popped out of a cave?

SINCHI Roca, MANCO Capac's SON, was the Inca's second LORD. Sinchi was much more PEACEFUL than his father. He was STYLISH and spent less time MURDERING people and more time inventing things. His greatest INVENTION was something that would show all the people, at a glance, who the royal family were—a special HAIRCUT! After Sinchi DIED, he was the first of the Inca lords to be turned into a MUMMY. Sinchi's CORPSE was kept so well it was put on show in CUZCO two HUNDRED years after his DEATH. Find the words in CAPITALS in the grid. The words can be found written up, down, forwards and backwards.

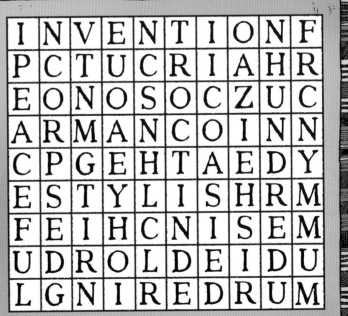

I	N	V	E	N	T	I	O	N	F
P	C	T	U	C	R	I	A	H	R
E	O	N	O	S	O	C	Z	U	C
A	R	M	A	N	C	O	I	N	N
C	P	G	E	H	T	A	E	D	Y
E	S	T	Y	L	I	S	H	R	M
F	E	I	H	C	N	I	S	E	M
U	D	R	O	L	D	E	I	D	U
L	G	N	I	R	E	D	R	U	M

The letters remaining will spell out what Sinchi's special haircut was called.

_ _ _ _ _ _ _ _ _ _ _

45

THE INCAS RULE

Up to this point, the eight Inca lords had ruled only the small area known as Cuzco. Now they wanted more land, more wealth and more people to push around. They weren't happy with just a valley, or even a country. They wanted a whole empire and the next Inca lord, a lad called Pachacuti, was just the man for the job.

> The next Inca leader, Pachacuti's son, Topa Inca Yupanqui, was topa the pops when it came to ruling. He and his dad made some nice new rules for the Incas to follow. Can you rearrange the letters to read the top ten Inca commandments?

THE TEN INCA COMMANDMENTS

1) Cuzco will be the CAT PAIL [capital] of the Incan RIPE ME.

2) The LEE POP will make the Cuzco valley farms the greatest DO OF producer ever.

3) A dead emperor's lands will be DASHER out amongst his AIM FLY. Each new emperor must conquer new lands of his own.

4) Conquered peoples will be CAR TESTED around the Incan Empire to work for the Incas.

5) Girls of conquered RIB SET may become chosen ME OWN to serve in the Incan temples or to marry great Incan RED SILOS.

6) A number of conquered men will be CON SHE to serve in the Incan MARY.

7) Everyone, including conquered peoples, will SHOW RIP the Incan DOG, [god] Viracocha.

8) Only the emperor may marry his RESIST.

9) The emperor may marry as many women as he SEWS HI, but no other man may. The lower your class, the fewer VIEWS you may have.

10) To speak to the emperor you must take off your LAND ASS and place a small load on your back as a sign of SPECTRE.

46

In 1438 the Chancas attacked the Incas. Pachacuti defeated the Chancas and said that the rocks of the hills turned into Inca warriors and cut the Chancas into pieces. Enemies were scared, and the Incas made the most of this fear. They piled sacred stones onto a platform and carried them into battle. Many enemies took one look at the rocks and gave up without a fight! Can you match the picture of sacred stones with the correct silhouette?

When Emperor Topa died, his son, Huayna, had to go out and conquer new land for himself. Huayna picked on the country we now call Ecuador, to the north of the country. All was going well, until Huayna heard about a deadly plague sweeping the country in Cuzco. And what did the idiot Inca do? He rushed back to Cuzco, caught the plague and died! Can you guide Huayna and his family through the mountain back to Cuzco?

CHILD'S PLAY

So the Incas became more powerful and their empire got bigger, but what was life like for an Inca child? Well, for a start, the more children and wives your father had, the more workers he had to produce food and to increase his power. So chances are, you had lots and lots of brothers, half-brothers, sisters and half-sisters – fun!

Peasant children were kept busy making beer and rounding up llamas and didn't go to school. If you were a lord's child you would have studied knotted string (Quipus – used to record information and events), the Inca language (Quechua), religion and history. Of course, you could make school more fun by messing about, but be warned, the punishment was pretty nasty. Can you add the missing words to find out more?

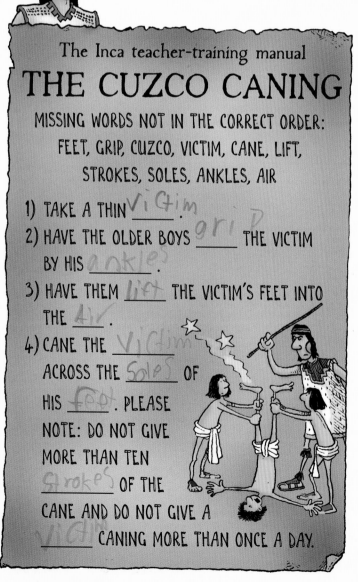

The Inca teacher-training manual
THE CUZCO CANING

MISSING WORDS NOT IN THE CORRECT ORDER:
FEET, GRIP, CUZCO, VICTIM, CANE, LIFT, STROKES, SOLES, ANKLES, AIR

1) TAKE A THIN ___victim___.
2) HAVE THE OLDER BOYS ___grip___ THE VICTIM BY HIS ___ankles___.
3) HAVE THEM ___lift___ THE VICTIM'S FEET INTO THE ___Air___.
4) CANE THE ___victim___ ACROSS THE ___Soles___ OF HIS ___feet___. PLEASE NOTE: DO NOT GIVE MORE THAN TEN ___Strokes___ OF THE CANE AND DO NOT GIVE A ___victim___ CANING MORE THAN ONCE A DAY.

For girls who didn't fancy housework and making beer, there was always the possibility of becoming a 'Chosen Woman'. Answer true or false to the questions below to see if you've got what it takes to become one.

1) The Inca name for Chosen Woman is – Quechua Aclla Cuna.

2) To apply, you have to talk to the patron (Papa Cuna) of the local temple.

3) All a girl needs is to be beautiful, clever and aged between 13 and 16 years.

4) Simple tasks of a Chosen Woman include cooking the holy food, keeping the sacred fire going and weaving the Emperor's temple clothes.

5) Specially selected Chosen Women may leave the temple to marry their fathers.

6) Lucky Chosen Women end up being burned as a temple sacrifice.

7) The terrible punishment for a Chosen Woman becoming pregnant is to be buried alive, unless she says the sun is the father of her baby.

8) By the 1500s there were 423 Chosen Women.

And for boys growing into men, the Incas had a special treat. Instead of a birthday party, they had an Incan initiation. Here is a game for you and a friend to play. Take turns rolling a dice and move the number of spaces shown. The first to reach the end will safely enter the world of the adult Inca male.

START 1

2 THERE'S GOING TO BE A SACRIFICE FOR THE INITIATION. THROW A 2 TO CONTINUE.

3 FOR THE SACRIFICE, YOU'VE KILLED A GUINEA PIG INSTEAD OF A LLAMA. MISS A TURN.

4

5 YOU'VE FOUND A LLAMA FOR THE SACRIFICE AND SNEAK UP QUIETLY. GO FORWARD 5.

6

7

16

15 YOU ROAST THE LLAMA MEAT, BUT FORGET TO SKIN THE ANIMAL. GO BACK TO THE START.

14

13 YOU CAN'T GET THE FIRE STARTED TO ROAST THE LLAMA MEAT. GO BACK 5.

12 YOU'VE SUCCESSFULLY SACRIFICED THE LLAMA. GO FORWARD 6.

11

10 CENSORED!

9 YUCK

17

18

19 YOU OFFER THE MEAT TO THE MOON GOD. GO BACK 3.

20

21

22

YUM!

24 YOU OFFER THE MEAT TO THE SUN GOD. GO FORWARD 5.

32

31 YOU'VE WHIPPED YOURSELF TO DRIVE OUT YOUR MANHOOD. GO FORWARD 7.

30

29 OW! AGH! OUCH! HOP IT, BOYHOOD!

28

27 YOU'VE TAKEN ALL YOUR CLOTHES OFF – YOU'RE ONLY MEANT TO STRIP TO THE WAIST. GO BACK 5.

26

25

33

34

35

36 YOU HAVE A FOOT RACE TO SHOW OFF YOUR SPEED AGAINST THE OTHER MEN. YOU COME IN LAST. GO BACK TO THE START.

37

38

39 PUFF! PANT!

40 YOU'VE LOST YOUR NEW WEAPONS – A SLING, A SHIELD AND A CLUB. GO BACK 6.

48

47 OW! ME EARS!

46 YOU GET YOUR EARS PIERCED SO EVERYONE CAN SEE YOU ARE NO LONGER A BOY. GO FORWARD 5.

45

44

43

42 YOU GET YOUR TONGUE PIERCED RATHER THAN YOUR EARS. MISS A TURN.

41

49

50 CONGRATULATIONS. YOU'VE GOT A NEW NAME. GO FORWARD 3.

51

52

53

54 YOU LOST YOUR NEW BREECHCLOTH. GO BACK 6.

55

FINISH CONGRATULATIONS! YOU'VE MADE IT – YOU'RE A MAN.

FOUL FASHION

Incan people were told what they should wear … just like school. You had to dress right for your class – you couldn't be a peasant and dress too posh! So you may think you know all there is to know about fashion, but the Incas could certainly teach you a thing or two about hairstyles and piercings.

So what does a fashionable male and female peasant wear? Look at the pictures below to find out. Can you spot the ten differences between these pairs of peasants and circle them with a pencil? But be careful, there may be some differences in the text too!

MEN — WOMEN

A LARGE CLOAK OVER THE SHOULDERS TIED IN THE FRONT. (THE FINER THE CLOTH AND EMBROIDERY, THE HIGHER YOUR CLASS.)

A SLEEVELESS TUNIC

A BREECH-CLOTH

A SHOULDER MANTLE

A WRAPAROUND SKIRT THAT REACHED FROM BENEATH THE ARMS TO THE ANKLES, WITH THE TOP EDGES DRAWN OVER THE SHOULDERS AND FASTENED WITH STRAIGHT PINS.

A DECORATED SASH

MEN — WOMEN

A LARGE CLOAK UNDER THE SHOULDERS TIED IN THE FRONT. (THE FINER THE CLOTH AND EMBROIDERY, THE HIGHER YOUR CLASS.)

A SLEEVELESS TUNIC

A BREECH-MOTH

A SHOULDER MANTLE

A WRAPAROUND SHIRT THAT REACHED FROM BENEATH THE ARMS TO THE ANKLES, WITH THE TOP EDGES DRAWN OVER THE SHOULDERS AND FASTENED WITH STRAIGHT TINS.

A DECORATED SASH

Girls! Now that you look like an Incan woman, you need to dress your hair like one. Collect some pee and leave it to brew for a week. Now soak your hair in the pee. When the hair is dry, start making it into braids – easy! Can you work out which buckets of pee these girls are washing their hair in?

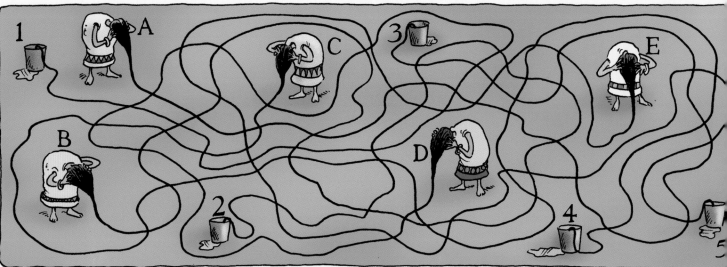

LIVE LIKE AN INCA

The Inca family groups were called 'ayllu' and the head of a large family was called a 'curaca'. A curaca was male and had power over everyone in the family. That meant Inca men ruled while women worked hard and had children.

There was very little crime in Inca villages and towns. Everyone shared what they owned, so there was no point in stealing! But the Incas did have 'set' punishments for certain crimes. Would you make a good Inca law enforcer? See if you can match these five crimes to the punishments.

...FOR THE CRIME OF...

1. KILLING AN ASSISTANT, IF YOU'RE A GOVERNMENT WORKER

2. BEING A WITCH OR WIZARD

3. REBELLION AGAINST THE STATE

4. GOING AGAINST THE LAWS OF THE GODS

5. TREASON AGAINST THE EMPEROR

THE PUNISHMENT WAS...

A. GIVEN A SLOW AND AGONIZING DEATH AND THEIR BONES TURNED INTO MUSICAL INSTRUMENTS

TOOT!

B. BEATEN TO DEATH AND THE BODY LEFT TO BE EATEN BY GIANT BIRDS CALLED CONDORS

C. BURNED ALIVE, HAVING HIS HOUSE BURNED TO THE GROUND, THE TREES UPROOTED AND THE CROPS DESTROYED

D. PLACED IN A CAVE FULL OF DANGEROUS ANIMALS FOR TWO DAYS

GRR!

OOOER!

E. LAID FACE DOWN ON THE GROUND AND A STONE DROPPED FROM A METRE HIGH ONTO THE BACK

1 =
2 =
3 =
4 =
5 =

What the Incas did each day depended on their age. They were divided into one of twelve classes. Can you tell which class each of these group of Incas belong to? Add the correct class number to the circles.

Class 1) **Babies** (in arms) and Class 2) **Infants** (up to one year): In the care of their parent.

Class 3) **Children** (aged 1-9): Children aged 1-5 may play. Children aged 5-9 must help parents in small tasks. At age 5 girls must start to learn how to weave. Girls planning to be servants will be sent away to be trained.

Class 4) **Youths** (aged 9-16): Boys will train as *llamamechecs* (llama herders of the llama herds). Girls are allowed to marry at 14.

Class 5) **Young men** (aged 16-20) and Class 6) **Prime men** (aged between 20-25): Will work as post-runners, senior llama herdsmen and as servants to military officers.

Class 7) **Young women** (aged 18-30): At this age they should be wives and mothers.

Class 8) *Puric* (men 25-50): This age group of men should be married. They must learn to farm their given piece of land and pay taxes and serve in the army if they are called to.

Class 9) **Unmarried women and widows** (aged 30-50): They will make pottery and cloth, and work as house-servants.

Class 10) **Old Men** (aged 50-60): These men are semi-retired and have no state or army duties. They are expected to help out from time to time during harvest and planting seasons, or to do light work as public officers, clerks and storekeepers.

Class 11) **Elders** (aged 60-80): Both men and women will eat, sleep, and may do light work if they are up to it, such as tending guinea pigs.

Class 12) **Invalids** (sick and disabled).

CURES AND ILLNESSES

The Incas were a fairly healthy people with no plague-type diseases …
until the conquistadors (Spanish conquerors) brought them over from Spain.
There were diseases like measles or smallpox that killed many Incas!
But the Incas did have some illnesses of their own … and some weird ways
to treat them that your local doctor would probably not advise today!

*Village healers used a special trick to make sick people believe
they were cured. They hypnotized the patient into a trance and
pretended to open up their stomach with a knife and pull out various
things. Copy the picture boxes into the grid to find out what creatures
this healer appears to be pulling out of the patient's stomach.*

1	2	3	4	5
6	7	8	9	10
11	12	13	14	15
16	17	18	19	20

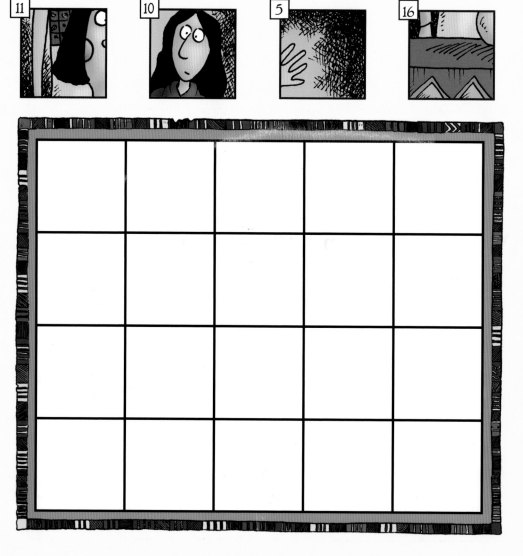

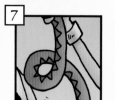

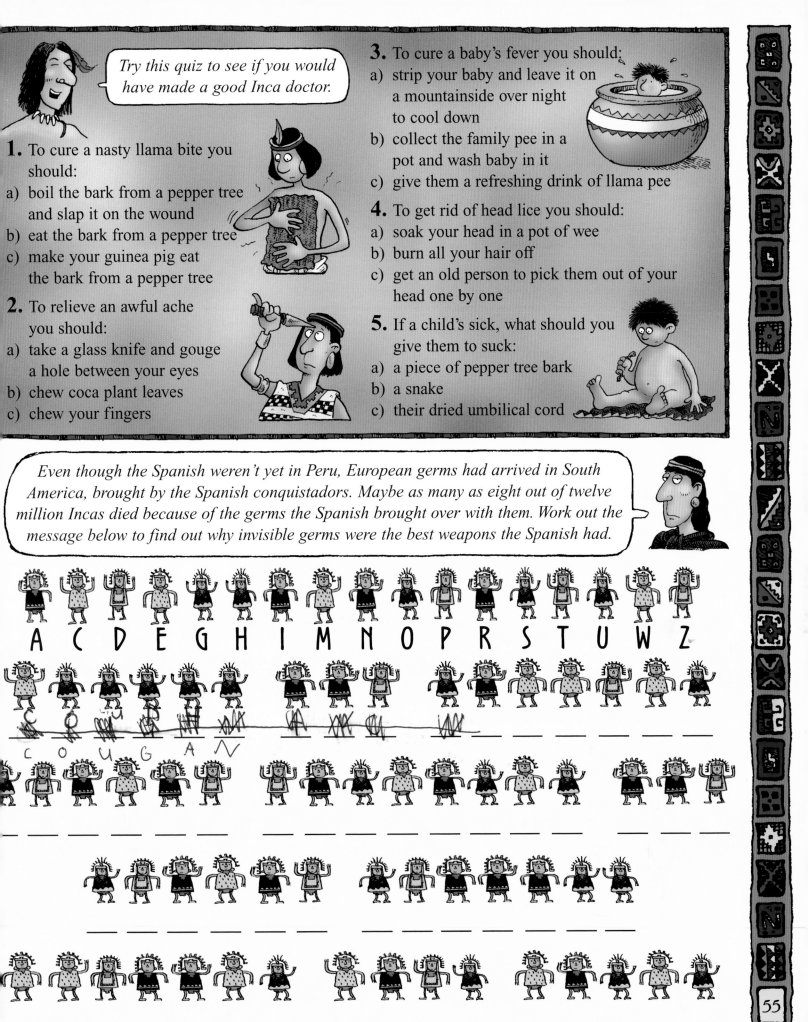

Try this quiz to see if you would have made a good Inca doctor.

1. To cure a nasty llama bite you should:
a) boil the bark from a pepper tree and slap it on the wound
b) eat the bark from a pepper tree
c) make your guinea pig eat the bark from a pepper tree

2. To relieve an awful ache you should:
a) take a glass knife and gouge a hole between your eyes
b) chew coca plant leaves
c) chew your fingers

3. To cure a baby's fever you should:
a) strip your baby and leave it on a mountainside over night to cool down
b) collect the family pee in a pot and wash baby in it
c) give them a refreshing drink of llama pee

4. To get rid of head lice you should:
a) soak your head in a pot of wee
b) burn all your hair off
c) get an old person to pick them out of your head one by one

5. If a child's sick, what should you give them to suck:
a) a piece of pepper tree bark
b) a snake
c) their dried umbilical cord

Even though the Spanish weren't yet in Peru, European germs had arrived in South America, brought by the Spanish conquistadors. Maybe as many as eight out of twelve million Incas died because of the germs the Spanish brought over with them. Work out the message below to find out why invisible germs were the best weapons the Spanish had.

A C D E G H I M N O P R S T U W Z

C O U G A N

FOUL FOOD

Hot, dry weather meant that crops were often poor, water was precious and people often starved. So what did the Inca lords do? They trained their people to fight and go out and pinch food and water from others!

When the Incas had a festival they enjoyed large amounts of their 'chicha' beer. Have you got a school assembly coming up? Need a cup or two of chicha to give you strength? Follow the simple (but disgusting) Incan instructions … on the other hand, you may prefer to stick to lemonade – without the spit! Some of the words have been replaced by pictures, to make it a bit more of a challenge!

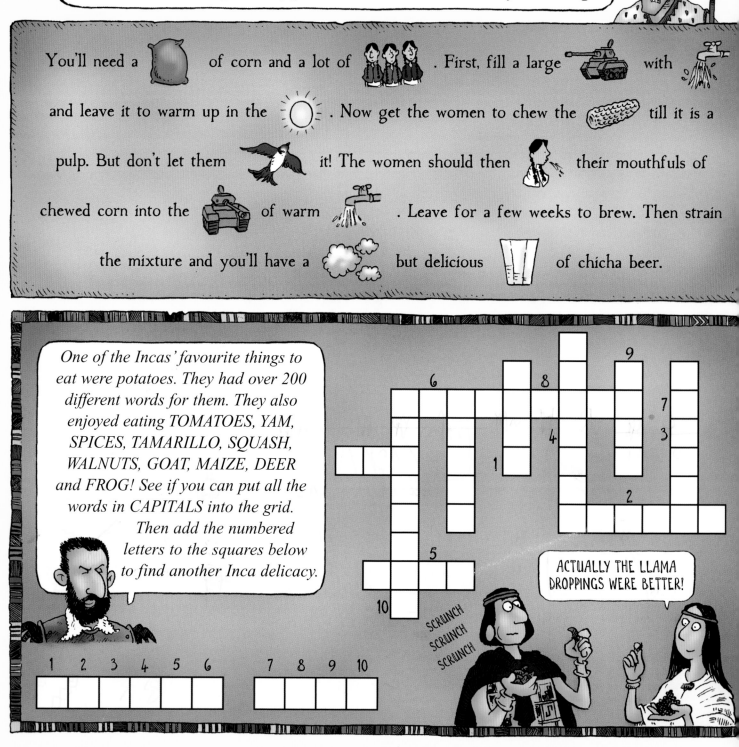

You'll need a [sack] of corn and a lot of [women]. First, fill a large [tank] with [tap]

and leave it to warm up in the [sun]. Now get the women to chew the [corn] till it is a

pulp. But don't let them [swallow] it! The women should then [spit] their mouthfuls of

chewed corn into the [tank] of warm [water]. Leave for a few weeks to brew. Then strain

the mixture and you'll have a [cloudy] but delicious [glass] of chicha beer.

One of the Incas' favourite things to eat were potatoes. They had over 200 different words for them. They also enjoyed eating TOMATOES, YAM, SPICES, TAMARILLO, SQUASH, WALNUTS, GOAT, MAIZE, DEER and FROG! See if you can put all the words in CAPITALS into the grid. Then add the numbered letters to the squares below to find another Inca delicacy.

ACTUALLY THE LLAMA DROPPINGS WERE BETTER!

SCRUNCH SCRUNCH SCRUNCH

| 1 | 2 | 3 | 4 | 5 | 6 | | 7 | 8 | 9 | 10 |

GODS AND SACRIFICES

The Incas worshipped many gods who required seriously savage sacrifices to keep them happy. Inca gods could be grim and gruesome – like a lot of gods in a lot of countries. Very often, a sacrifice was simply a way of saying 'Thank you!'

So, who were some of these gods? Well, Inti was the Sun god, Viracocha (also known as Lord Instructor of the World, The Ancient One and the Old Man of the Sky), was Creator of Earth, humans and animals and Mama-Kilya was the moon mother and wife of Inti. Draw the picture of the three gods by copying the lines in each square onto the empty grid.

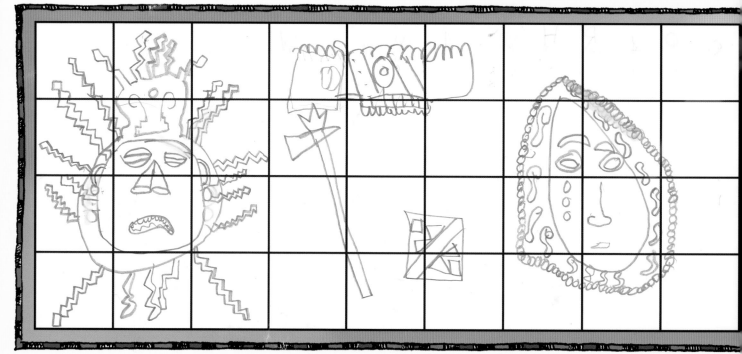

58

The magnificent Sun Temple was where sacrifices to the sun god were made. The temple was a gold-plated palace, 100 metres long and 30 metres wide. But sacrifices weren't just made in temples, and there were different sacrifices for different occasions. Can you match the right occasion with the sacrifice?

OCCASION

1) Before a big battle
2) On the first day of every month
3) To make the sun appear every day
4) At a wedding
5) To keep the gods happy

SACRIFICE

A) 2 'red' llamas
B) 1000s of llamas
C) 100 pure white llamas
D) 1 innocent child
E) Corn

ANSWERS

1) =
2) =
3) =
4) =
5) =

HOW A-LLAMING!

The Incas sacrificed children at the top of mountains. A child sacrifice was payment to the mountain god for the sun and rain. Some of the victims have been found with strange shaped heads. It seems that wood had been strapped to their heads from birth, so the infant heads were forced to grow to a point! The head took on the shape of the mountain on which they'd be sacrificed. Which path will lead the child to the mountain?

FOOL'S GOLD

By 1532, the Incas had conquered dozens of states and ruled over 12 million people who spoke at least 20 different languages. The Incan empire was enormous. But thanks to Christopher Columbus, the Spanish had discovered America. And once a conquistador called Francisco Pizarro had landed, the Incas power started to come to an end.

The Incas said they lived in Tahuantinsuyu. So how come the SPANISH arrived and called it PERU? Well, in 1511, the Spanish conquistador, BALBOA, was WEIGHING some gold when a young AMERINDIAN chieftain STRUCK the SCALES with his FIST. He said that he could tell Balboa where he could find a LAND where GOLD was as CHEAP as IRON and people ate from golden PLATES and DRANK from GOLDEN CUPS. Balboa asked where he could find this land and the CHIEFTAIN told him '_____' meaning, 'What you want is over there, keep going and going and going!' But the Spanish thought they were being directed to a COUNTRY named 'Peru'! To find out what the Chieftain actually said, find the words in CAPITALS in the grid below. The words can be found written up, down, forwards and backwards.

A	C	S	T	R	U	C	K	H	B
M	H	D	S	E	L	A	C	S	G
E	E	L	D	R	A	N	K	I	N
R	A	O	N	N	O	R	I	N	I
I	P	G	A	T	S	I	F	A	H
N	E	D	L	O	G	I	R	P	G
D	R	B	A	L	B	O	A	S	I
I	U	S	E	T	A	L	P	P	E
A	C	O	U	N	T	R	Y	U	W
N	I	A	T	F	E	I	H	C	U

The letters remaining will spell out what the Chieftain said: ___ ___ ___ ___

So who was this Francisco Pizarro (or Franny to you and me)? With his 250 men, he conquered millions of Incas. Here are some fascinating facts about him. Answer true or false.

FRANNY'S FANTASTIC FACTS

1) Franny grew up in France.
2) Franny's job was to look after the pigs.
3) It is said that his parents ran away and left him. He survived because he was brought up by a sow.
4) Franny used a stencil made of his name and coloured it in when he needed to sign a paper.

AND I'M USING A DIFFERENT COLOUR FOR EACH LETTER!

THAT'S MY BOY!

5) Franny joined the explorer Nunez de Balboa when he crossed Panama and discovered the Pacific Ocean in 1513.
6) Franny then joined up with the soldier Diego de Almagro and they set off to conquer lands north of Panama.
7) On one of his expeditions, Franny was wounded 27 times.

Francisco Pizarro wanted to get his hands on some of the Inca wealth. He took the Incan Emperor Atahuallpa prisoner and held him to ransom. That way, he could get the Inca people to bring their treasure to him. The Incas agreed. Treasure came from all corners of the 2,000 mile empire – 13,265 pounds (6,017 kilos) of gold and 26 pounds (12 kilos) of silver. But Pizarro didn't release Atahuallpa – he killed him instead. Can you spot the ten differences between the two pictures and circle them with a pencil?

CONQUERING CONQUISTADORS

The Incan armies were lost without Atahuallpa, and Pizarro's small group of conquistadors went on to conquer millions of Incas. The rest, as they say, is history.

Help Pizarro and his army round up the Incas in the right order – from 1 to 10. Remember, you can't go over the same path twice.

Of course the Incas tried to rebel against Spanish rule from time to time. But not very successfully! At one uprising, the Inca fighters taunted the Spanish by lifting their bare legs at them! Which of the numbered pictures below are from the main image?

WE'RE MAKING A STAND

Once the Spanish were in charge the Inca peasants became slaves, working with just enough food to keep them alive. The greatest suffering was in the silver mines. Pick one of the Inca slaves and see if you will survive to work another month.

A   B   C   D

You breathed in too much of the poisonous mercury and died a slow, agonising death.

You sweated so much filling your cloak with rocks that you died of pneumonia when you dragged the rocks to the surface and the cold air hit you.

You were transferred to a sugar cane factory and were crushed to death by the heavy machinery that crushed the cane.

Well done! You survive another month working in the mine and earn a piece of cloth for your trouble.

63

GRISLY QUIZ

So you think you now know a thing or two about the awesome ancients? Test your knowledge with this multiple choice quiz and see if you're a *Horrible Histories* expert or not.

The awesome Egyptians

1. What percentage of Egyptians lived as slaves, er, sorry, peasants? (Of course, they might as well have been slaves!)
   a) 20%   **b)** 40%   **c)** 90%

2. The pharaoh proved his fitness to be king by doing one of the following trials:
   a) killing at least 100 enemies by his own hand within the first five years of his reign
   b) running round a gruelling obstacle course after he'd reigned for 30 years
   c) having at least four children by the end of the tenth year of his reign

3. Gods played a very important role in Egyptian life. Which of these three is actually an Egyptian god?
   a) Re – the Sun God. Some said he made people. The Egyptians called themselves, 'the cattle of Re'.
   b) Ta – the Moon God. Egyptians would howl to Ta when the moon was full.
   c) Bla – the god of the universe. Egyptians made animal sacrifices to him twice a month.

4. Egyptians spent most of their lives worrying about:
   a) taxes
   b) the plague
   c) the afterlife

5. The Egyptians who could read and write were called:
   a) wordsmiths   **b)** scribes   **c)** editors

6. Why did Egyptians make their dead (at least the ones who could afford it) into mummies?
   a) to scare away grave robbers
   b) bodies that rotted wouldn't make it into the afterlife
   c) to keep the rats from nibbling on their toes

7. How many pyramids were built in ancient Egypt?
   a) 35   **b)** 96   **c)** 57

8. What happened to certain body parts that were taken out of a dead body?
   a) They were put into canopic jars.
   b) They were thrown into the River Nile.
   c) They were burned at the entrance to the pyramid.

9. What do many people believe happened when you robbed a pharaoh's tomb?
   a) The ceiling would collapse on top of you.
   b) You would be cursed by the mummy and probably die.
   c) Your brain would turn to jelly.

The groovy Greeks

10. The great playwright, Aeschylus, is supposed to have died when an eagle flew over his head and dropped something on it. What did the eagle drop?

a) a tortoise

b) a hare

c) a stone

11. What is a Doric Chiton?

a) a sharp knife

b) an early kite made out of papyrus and hemp

c) a type of tunic

12. The Greeks invented a new weapon in the 4th century BC. They set fire to inflammable liquids then threw them over enemy ships or enemy cities. What is this weapon called?

a) Greek fire

b) Zeus's revenge

c) flaming dangerous

13. A sacred plant was sprinkled on graves. We don't consider it sacred today. What is it?

a) cabbage

b) parsley

c) garlic

14. What did the Greek gods eat?

a) ambrosia

b) ancient Greeks

c) aubergines

15. As well as the Olympic games, there were games in Isthmia. The winners at the Isthmian games were given a crown as a prize. What was the crown made of?

a) rhubarb

b) celery

c) gold

16. The Greek god of wine and merry-making was the grooviest god of all. What was his name?

a) Didymus

b) Dionysus

c) Dipymus

17. Draco wrote the first law books for the Athenians. Which statement is true?

a) You could have someone made your personal slave if they owed you money.

b) If you stole an apple or a cabbage, you were sentenced to death.

c) People found guilty of idleness would be executed.

18. Before clever Aristotle came along, the Greeks had a strange belief about elephants. What was it?

a) An elephant has no knee joints so it goes to sleep leaning against a tree.

b) Elephants never forget.

c) Eating elephant makes you strong.

19. The poet Homer described a race between Achilles and Odysseus (who was losing). He said a prayer to Athena who made Achilles slip and fall into...

a) cattle droppings

b) a puddle

c) a hole in the ground

The incredible Incas

20. The Inca people liked to keep their dead kings happy. How?

a) They fed them lots of beer so they could be Inca drinkas.

b) They put the latest books in the grave so they could be Inca thinkas.

c) They changed the shoes on the kingly corpses every week because they didn't want them to be Inca stinkas.

THIS IS THE LIFE!

21. Inca Huaca was released by the conquistadors who captured him because he, what?

a) Cut their hair

b) Cooked them dinner

c) Cried

22. We call everyone who lived in the Empire 'Incas' today. But in those days 'Inca' was a word that was used for what?

a) Only the men (because women didn't matter).

b) Only the royal family (because no one else mattered).

c) Only the people of Cuzco (because conquered people didn't matter).

23. What nickname did the Spanish conquistadors give to the Incas when they first met them?

a) Noddies   **b)** Mr Plods   **c)** Big Ears

I HEARD THAT!

BIG EARS!

24. When an Inca killed an enemy what could he use the dead man's skin for?

a) To cover a drum … so the enemy would be beaten twice! (Boom! Boom!)

b) To wrap some sandwiches for the journey home.

c) To scrape thin enough to let light through and use as a window in the family home.

BRILLIANT! THERE'S ENOUGH HERE FOR DOUBLE GLAZING!

25. Which of these three facts is FALSE?

a) The Incas enjoyed popcorn.

b) Old people were given the job of collecting lice.

c) The Incas rode on llamas.

26. Incas had many different ways of finding out about the future, one of which was to:

a) Watch the way a spider wandered across the floor.

b) Sort through a guinea pig's droppings looking for clues.

c) Ride a blind llama round the temple twenty times.

THAT'S GOT TO BE A BAD SIGN!

SPLAT!

OW!

27. Cuzco was 4,000 metres above sea level where the air is thin and most humans would struggle to breathe. How did the Incas manage?

a) They had really big strong hearts for pumping what little oxygen there was around their bodies.

b) They had big noses and big mouths so they could gulp down more air than most people.

c) They had big air tanks like aqualungs (made from llama skin) that they filled each day with lowland air and carried home to breathe.

ANSWER PAGES

PAGES 4-5: WHAT IS AN AWESOME EGYPTIAN?

There were few slaves in Egypt…

30 peasants and cattle work on Ali Fayed's land. Remember, women were not counted.

When the Nile was in flood…

Peasant C faces the chop.

Some peasants who worked hard…

Unscrambled words in the correct order: STONE BLOCKS, BURNING DESERT, BREAD, OINTMENT, LIMESTONE, MUD FLOORS, CROWDED, WATER, TOILETS, STUNK, SEWAGE, ANIMALS, STARVATION.

PAGES 6-7: WRITE LIKE AN EGYPTIAN

See if you can read these two…

Pyramids ar(e) big   My nits ar(e) itchy

If you think school is bad…

Unscrambled words in the correct order: IDLE, CURSED, NOT, HEART, PLEASURE, SHALL, SPEND, IDLENESS, BEATEN, BOY'S, BACKSIDE, WHEN, BEATEN!

Can you find the list of these…

1) GIZA
2) SAND
3) CHARM
4) RING
5) INK
6) SPIRITS

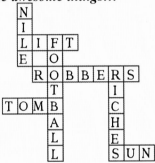

PAGES 8-9: GRUESOME GODS

Egyptian gods were unbelievably…

1 = J	2 = G	3 = K	4 = A	5 = C	6 = H
7 = E	8 = B	9 = L	10 = I	11 = F	12 = D

Need an awesome answer to a powerful problem?

1 = Sobek   2 = Isis   3 = Thoth   4 = Sekhmet   5 = Hathor

Most awesome Egyptian myths…

Unscrambled words in the correct order: JEALOUS, ORGANISED, ANNOUNCED, SEALED, SEARCHED, BURIAL, ANGERED, SCATTERED, WRAPPED.

PAGES 10-11: PHASCINATING PHARAOHS

Pharaohs ruled for almost 3,000 years…

1 = WOMAN   2 = MURDER   3 = WRINKLY
4 = HUNDRED   5 = MAGICIAN   6 = GOOSE
7 = LION   8 = ELEPHANTS   9 = MONEY   10 = GREEK

After ruling for 30 years…

The carvings on all Egyptian…

PAGES 12-13: POWERFUL PYRAMIDS

There are some awesome things…

(crossword: NILE, LIFT, FOOTBALL, ROBBERS, TOMB, RICHES, SUN)

Not everyone agrees the pyramids are…

All except number 3 have been believed by someone.

The biggest pyramid is the…

The word PYRAMID can be seen 7 times in the grid.

PAGES 14-15: POTTY PYRAMIDS

Can you find the words listed in…

The *Awesome Egyptians* lived 5,000 years ago!

Archaeologists in Egypt…

There are 35 overlapping pyramids.

PAGES 16-17: MAGICAL MUMMIES

The men who made dead bodies…

Instructions in the correct order: D, F, J, B, A, E, H, C, I, G.

The following mummies will tell you…

1, 2, 4, 5, 6 & 7 = TRUE   3 = FALSE

PAGES 18-19: FATE OF THE MUMMY

The monsters that live in the Duat…

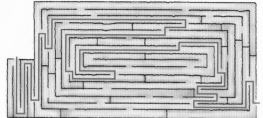

At the gates of Yaru…   The Egyptians mummified more…

 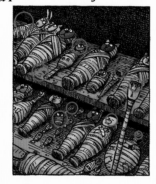

Pilgrims came to ancient Egypt like…

1 = RABBIT   2 = FISH   3 = DOG   4 = PIG   5 = DUCK
Pilgrims bought mummified CATS as souvenirs.

PAGES 20-21: GRUESOME GRAVE-ROBBERS

Cast yourself back in time…

1 = No. You will need a group of at least 7 or 8 people to help you.
2 = Yes. They will help you to enter the tomb and open the coffin.
3 = No. You should find a back entrance. With the front entrance untouched, no one will suspect anything's wrong.
4 = Yes. You will need the officials and priests to turn a blind eye.
5 = Yes. The gold will be melted down, ready for you to move it easily.
6 = No. Merchants can buy your stolen treasures – no questions asked.
7 = No. Many a grave-robber was caught this way. People wanted to know where all that wealth came from.
8 = No. You need to know the passages and rooms as well as a tomb builder.
9 = Yes. It could save you a lot of trouble.
10 = Yes. You will be tortured and then executed.

Pharaohs eventually realised that…

Many tomb-builders became grave-robbers…

PAGES 22-23: CURIOUS CURSES

Lots of 'true' mummy stories have been told…

Story in the correct sequence:
G, A, M, H, B, I, C,
F, L, N, D, J, K, O, E

Lord Carnarvon ignored his friend's…

The death of Lord Carnarvon was…

1 = True, but… Mace had been ill before he entered the tomb. He had pleurisy. There were no cures for this illness in 1922.
2 = Lies. A newspaper reported this curse soon after Carnarvon's death.
3 = True, but it's a creepy story told by Lord Carnarvon's son.
4 = Lies. The British Museum never had any objects from Tut's tomb.
5 = Mistake. Gould was not in good health before his visit. He went to Egypt because he was ill, but the stress of travelling killed him.
6 = Mistake. The air in the tomb wouldn't be very healthy, but King Tut's germs wouldn't kill a visitor.

PAGES 24-25: WHO WERE THE GROOVY GREEKS?

Here's a quick quiz to see…

1 = NAY   2 = YEA   3 = YEA   4 = YEA   5 = YEA
1) They threw him off the top of a cliff.
2) Not only were children sacrificed, but bits of them were eaten, too.
5) This was a popular story told by Spartans. It was probably one big fib.

The Greeks were very groovy with…

Teachers don't know everything, they just try to kid you that they do.

The Greeks invented some crazy customs…

1 = BOTH   2 = A FUNERAL   3 = BOTH
4 = A FUNERAL   5 = BOTH   6 = BOTH   7 = BOTH
8 = A WEDDING   9 = BOTH   10 = A FUNERAL

PAGES 26-27: GRUESOME GODS

These new gods were just one…

1 = ZEUS = E   2 = POSEIDON = C   3 = HADES = A
4 = APHRODITE = D   5 = APOLLO = B
6 = ATHENA = F

The Greek myths are still popular today…

1 = f   2 = d   3 = c   4 = e   5 = b   6 = a

PAGES 28-29: FIGHT LIKE A GREEK

Everyone knows the story of…

Correct order of pictures: G, C, H, A, E, B, I, J, D, F

King Darius of Persia had a large…

16 Persian skulls   123 Egyptian skulls.
The Persians won the battle at Pelusium.

Can you work out which of these things…

1) SOAP = YES   2) CAMERA = NO   3) PARACHUTE = NO
4) ANCHOR = YES   5) CHEWING GUM = YES   6) SIREN = YES
7) CATAPULT = YES   8) SANDWICHES = NO
9) ROLLER SKATES = NO   10) SPECTACLES = NO
1) Made from goat fat and ashes.
2) Invented in Britain in the 1820's and 30's.
3) First jump was made from a hot air balloon in Britain, 1797.
5) The ancient Greeks chewed mastic gum – resin from the bark of the mastic tree, found mainly in Greece and Turkey. Used to clean their teeth and sweeten their breath.
8) The Romans first had the idea of eating meat between bread.
9) First seen in 1700's Britain. Joseph Merlin skated into a ballroom, playing a violin.
10) Invented around 1287 in Italy.

PAGES 30-31: SAVAGE SPARTANS

Life was extra-tough for Spartan…

1 = herd   2 = bite   3 = mountains   4 = hair
5 = beaten   6 = baths   7 = no clothes
1) The toughest child became leader and ordered the others about.
3) Sickly babies were left up a mountain to die.
5) Children were kept hungry and encouraged to steal food!
7) So they didn't get fancy ideas about fine clothes.

One Spartan general wanted to betray his…

1 = SPARTA   2 = DEFEAT   3 = PUNISHED
4 = ASSASSINS   5 = TRAITOR   6 = KING
7 = KILL   8 = HAUNT   9 = GHOST
The Spartan general was called PAUSANIUS.

Spartans lied, cheated and tricked their way…

PAGES 32-33: LIVE LIKE A GREEK

Being a female in ancient Greece…

1 = FALSE   2 = TRUE   3 = TRUE   4 = TRUE   5 = TRUE
6 = FALSE   7 = TRUE   8 = TRUE   9 = FALSE   10 = FALSE

Life was even worse for…

1 = a   2 = c   3 = b   4 = e   5 = d

PAGES 34-35: GROOVY GREEK GAMES

Here's a quick quiz to see how much…

1 = NAY   2 = YEA   3 = YEA   4 = YEA
5 = YEA   6 = NAY   7 = YEA   8 = YEA
1) They were given a pension, free meals and money.
6) They could be whipped or banned from future games.
7) This was a race in armour.

Can you find these words…

NIKE was the goddess of victory.

Not all Olympic champs died…

1 = b   2 = c   3 = a   4 = b   5 = a

PAGES 36-37: EVEN GROOVIER GREEK GAMES

In the game called…

PAGES 38-39: DIE LIKE A GREEK

Hippocrates was a…

Hippo took samples…

1 = Nasty no
2 = Yummy yes
3 = Nasty no
4 = Yummy yes
5 = Yummy yes
6 = Yummy yes
7 = Nasty no
8 = Yummy yes
9 = Nasty no
10 = Yummy yes

Not every doctor was as good as…

PAGES 40-41: FUNNY FOOD

A sacrifice is supposed to be…

1 = a   2 = a   3 = b   4 = c   5 = a   6 = b   7 = a

After about 500 BC…

1 = THRUSHES   2 = OVERFED PIGS   3 = SEA URCHINS
4 = YORKSHIRE PUDDING   5 = PEACOCK EGGS
6 = HONEY CAKES   7 = TURNIPS   8 = FLOWER SEEDS
9 = GRASSHOPPERS   10 = SPAGHETTI
The Greeks would have eaten them all except 4 and 10.

Milon was a wrestler…

PAGES 42-43: THINK LIKE A GREEK

At the Corinth Oracle…

People today are nervous about…

Missing words in the correct order: messengers, earth, moon, bodies, dead, disease, tar, reflection, die, spirits, protected, evil, wickedness.

Can you imagine your maths…

ALL TRUE!

How many of the following facts…

1) The Greek explorer, Pytheas, sailed to the North Sea.
2) The Greek teacher, Gorgias, was born in his dead mother's coffin.
3) Spartan youths trained in the secret police.
4) A Greek sportsman enjoyed the team sport called hockey.
5) The girls of Attica ran about naked in the woods pretending to be bears.
6) The Greek teacher, Pythagoras, believed you shouldn't touch a fire with an iron poker.
7) The Greek doctor, Aesculapius, cut off a girl's head to cure water on the brain.
8) General Alcibiades knocked off the naughty bits on the statues of Greek gods.

PAGES 44-45: MEET THE LEGENDARY INCA LORDS

Put the six pictures below in the…

Correct order of pictures: C, E, B, F, A, D

Can you match the questions with the…

1) = Sinchi Roca   2) = Viracocha   3) = Mayta Capac
4) = Yahuar Huacac   5) = Inca Roca   6) = Capac Yupanqui
7) = Lloque Yupanqui   8) = Manco Capac
8) It is said that there are three caves at Paqari-tampu where Manco Capac first saw the light of day, along with his three brothers and four sisters.

SINCHI Roca, MANCO…

Sinchi said that the Incan rulers would have their hair cut straight across the forehead. The haircut Sinchi invented was a *fringe*.

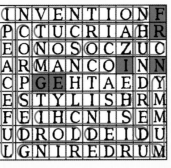

I	N	V	E	N	T	I	O	N	F
P	C	T	U	C	R	I	A	H	R
E	O	N	O	S	O	C	Z	U	O
A	R	M	A	N	C	O	I	N	N
C	P	G	E	H	T	A	E	D	Y
E	S	T	Y	L	I	S	H	R	M
F	E	C	H	C	N	I	S	E	M
U	D	R	O	L	D	E	I	D	U
L	G	N	I	R	E	D	R	U	M

PAGES 46-47: THE INCAS RULE

The next Inca leader, Pachacuti's son…

Unscrambled words in the correct order: capital, empire, people, food, shared, family, scattered, tribes, women, soldiers, chosen, army, worship, god, sister, wishes, wives, sandals, respect

In 1438 the Chancas attacked the…

Silhouette 3 matches the picture. As the Chancas ran away, hundreds of Inca supporters, living in the hills, ran down and attacked them. Yes, the Chancas were massacred in the hills, but not by rocks!

When Emperor Topa…

Huayna didn't name the next emperor, and then his son died a few days later. That left two half-brothers (Huascar and Atahuallpa) to fight one another for the throne. As they fought, the Incan empire was divided – just as Spanish invaders arrived. That's what made it so easy for the Spanish to defeat them.

PAGES 48-49: CHILD'S PLAY

Peasant children were kept busy making beer…

Missing words in the correct order: cane, grip, ankles, lift, air, victim, soles, feet, strokes, Cuzco

For girls who didn't fancy housework and…

1) = true   2) = false   3) = false   4) = true
5) = false   6) = true   7) = true   8) = false

2) Girls had to apply to the matron (Mama Cuna) of the local temple.
3) To be a Chosen Woman, a girl had to be between 8 and 10 years old.
5) Selected Chosen Women were allowed to leave to marry lords.
8) By the 1500s there were several thousand Chosen Women.

PAGES 50-51: FOUL FASHION

So what does a fashionable…

Girls! Now that you look…

A = 3   B = 2   C = 4   D = 1   E = 5

Male members of the Inca royal family and…

Inca 4 is trying to be the noblest. His ear weights add up to 10205g, all the other weights add up to 1 kilo (1000g).

PAGES 52-53: LIVE LIKE AN INCA

There was very little crime in Inca villages and…

1) = E   2) = B   3) = A   4) = C   5) = D

1) This sometimes killed the prisoner. If it didn't, then he was left with severe injuries for the rest of his life.
5) A conquistador once described this, 'In the cave of Sancay, prisoners convicted of treason were placed in a cavern full of wild animals, toxic toads and venomous reptiles. If a convict survived two days in these surroundings he was pardoned and released, since his survival seemed to signal that he was obviously under the protection of the gods.'

What the Incas did each day depended on their…

PAGES 54-55: CURES AND ILLNESSES

Village healers used a special trick to make…

The village healer is pretending to pull snakes and toads from the man's stomach. After this conjuring trick was over, the healer would clean the blood off the body and say, 'Look! The wound is healed and all this poison inside you is gone!' The patient would feel better because they really believed they'd been cured.

Try this quiz to see if you would…

1) = a   2) = a   3) = b   4) = c   5) = c

2) It seems that the hole-in-the-head treatment worked – it was meant to let evil spirits leave the body. Archaeologists have found skulls with pieces removed and it is clear the wound healed and the patient survived.

5) Sensible mothers cut their baby's umbilical cord when they were born and then dried and stored it. When sucked, it was meant to suck the pain and evil spirits away from the body.

Even though the Spanish weren't yet in Peru…

The message reads: coughs and sneezes spread diseases and spread Spanish empires with eases

PAGES 56-57: FOUL FOOD

When the Incas had a festival they enjoyed…

Missing words in the correct order: sack, women, tank, water, sun, corn, swallow, spit, tank, water, cloudy, glass

One of the Incas' favourite…

Another Inca delicacy was GUINEA PIGS.

PAGES 58-59: GODS AND SACRIFICES

The magnificent Sun Temple was where…

1) = B   2) = C   3) = E   4) = A   5) = D

The Incas sacrificed children at the top of…

PAGES 60-61: FOOL'S GOLD

The Incas said they lived…

The Amerindian chieftain said, 'Biru' not 'Peru'.

So who was this Francisco Pizarro…

1) = false 2) = true 3) = true 4) = true 5) = true 6) = false 7) = false

1) Franny grew up in Spain.

4) Frany used a stencil because he couldn't write.

6) Franny and Diego set off to conquer lands *south* of Panama.

7) Franny was wounded seven times.

Francisco Pizarro wanted to get his hands on some…

PAGES 62-63: CONQUERING CONQUISTADORS

Help Pizarro and his army round up the…

Of course the Incas tried to rebel…

1, 4, 5, 8 and 9 can be found in the main picture. This 'insult' is still used in the Andes. Insulting, perhaps – but not very effective!

Once the Spanish were in charge…

If you chose slave C, you would survive another month.

PAGES 64-66: GRISLY QUIZ

1 = c   2 = b   3 = a   4 = c   5 = b   6 = b   7 = b

8 = a   9 = b   10 = a   11 = c   12 = a   13 = b   14 = a

15 = b   16 = b   17 = a,b and c   18 = a   19 = a   20 = a

21 = c   22 = b   23 = c   24 = a   25 = c   26 = a   27 = a

21. Huaca cried tears of blood! His captors were amazed and set him free.

23. They called them Big Ears because of the way the Incas stretched their ear lobes to wear big ornaments.

24. The Incas went into battle playing drums and tambourines with the skin of dead enemies.

25. Llamas were used like donkeys to carry loads, but the Incas never rode them.

27. Inca hearts could carry 60% more blood round the body than the average human.